MAMA'S BOY

A YOUNG BOY'S MEMORY OF CHILDHOOD

Mama's Boy: A Young Boy's Memory Of Childhood
Copyright © 2024 by Rev. Michael H. Lavery

Published in the United States of America

Library of Congress Control Number: 2024916527
ISBN   Paperback: 979-8-89091-684-6
ISBN   eBook: 979-8-89091-685-3

All rights reserved. No part of this publication may be reproduced, stored in a retrieval system or transmitted in any way by any means, electronic, mechanical, photocopy, recording or otherwise without the prior permission of the author except as provided by USA copyright law.

The opinions expressed by the author are not necessarily those of ReadersMagnet, LLC.

ReadersMagnet, LLC
10620 Treena Street, Suite 230 | San Diego, California, 92131 USA
1.619. 354. 2643 | www.readersmagnet.com

Book design copyright © 2024 by ReadersMagnet, LLC. All rights reserved.

Cover design by Tifanny Curaza
Interior design by Don De Guzman

MAMA'S BOY

A YOUNG BOY'S MEMORY OF CHILDHOOD

Rev. Michael H. Lavery

TABLE OF CONTENTS

Foreword vii
Dedication ix

Chapter 1:   I Was Born A Fatherless Child 1
Chapter 2:   My Sissy's Smile 5
Chapter 3:   Mama Was An Angel 11
Chapter 4:   Living With The Lone Ranger 15
Chapter 5:   Then Came Jesus 25
Chapter 6:   Operation: Bring Our Parents To Jesus 43
Chapter 7:   Life Lessons 57
                Lesson 1: Santa Never Gives You Everything
                You Want. 57
                Lesson 2: Outward Appearance Can Be Deceiving ... 64
                Lesson 3: Is That The Best You Can Do? 76
                Lesson 4: A Real Man Never Strikes A Woman 83
                Lesson 5: A Real Man Takes Responsibility
                For His Actions 87
Chapter 8:   Gone, But Never Far Away 95

FOREWORD

By Rev. Michael H. Lavery

The words Mama's Boy are a source of great shame to most young men. It is not said as a compliment, but instead is meant as a slight. However, to me the term is a badge of honor.

When someone calls me a Mama's Boy, I stand a little straighter, my chest swells with pride. For me it is a badge of honor. Why, you ask? The answer is simple. The courage, honor and fidelity of the two women that raised my sister and me.

When you have finished this story, I am about to relate, you will understand why.

Thank you for sharing my journey.

DEDICATION

In grateful praise to our heavenly Father who in his wise providence, extended to me the privilege of being raised by two such extraordinary women.

CHAPTER 1

I WAS BORN A FATHERLESS CHILD

When I entered this world in September of Nineteen fifty-five, I was born a fatherless child.

In this present age, such an occurrence is by no means uncommon. For many young men today, producing a child in the biological sense almost seems to be a rite of passage into manhood.

While being capable of producing a child, these boys do not have the chops nor the intestinal fortitude to raise one.

The result of this folly is young children who will never experience the love of a committed father.

However, this was not to be my lot. My father, from all the accounts, was a good man. He loved my mother and adored my older sister, Kathy. He did not abandon us, and had he lived, I am quite sure he would have been a wonderful father to me.

Sadly, he did not live. This is where my narrative begins.

It was March sixth, nineteen fifty-five, my sister Kathy's first birthday. My mother had ordered a cake and had invited several close friends and family to help celebrate such a momentous occasion.

My father and mother were not only the proud parents of a one-year-old little girl but only recently discovered yet another bundle of joy was on its way.

From all accounts, my father adored children. My mother often told me that had he lived, there was no telling how many siblings I would have had.

My mother had struggled mightily bringing my sister into this world. The thought of her enduring another such ordeal was a cause of great concern for my dad.

On the morning of my sister's birthday, Mother escorted Dad to his streetcar stop. Dad did not own a car and took the streetcar to work every morning.

Back in the fifties, a good number of people did not own cars. The streetcar lines had a thriving business.

As they walked toward the stop my mother pleaded with my dad to take the day off work. This was a milestone birthday for Kathy. Family and friends would be coming, and Mother wanted Dad to be present when the cake was cut.

My father had a wonderful boss who was good to him and all the men that worked for him. Mother and Dad both knew that for an occasion as momentous as a first birthday, he would surely have given Dad the day off had he asked. However, my father had a very strong sense of responsibility. They had a big job, and all hands were needed. My father promised he would do his best to get off early.

The streetcar arrived right on time. Mother kissed Dad and once again he promised to come home early, if possible. My mother stood on the curb as the streetcar pulled away. What Dad did next took my mother by surprise. Dad made his way to the back of the streetcar and waved to my mother from the back window. He had never done that before. As she waved back, she had no way of knowing that she would never lay eyes on her beloved Pete again.

The day was a flurry of activity. Kathy had to be fed, the cake had to be picked up, and food had to be prepared for the party. Then the guests began to arrive. It was a joyful celebration. Mother held off cutting the cake and singing Happy Birthday in the hope my father would soon be home.

But as the hour grew late and my sister, deprived of her nap, became cranky. Mother decided to sing Happy Birthday and cut the cake. Family and friends sat around eating cake and conversing. Mother heard a knock at the door. She felt a sense of relief, my father must have forgotten his key again. However, when Mother opened the door, much to her surprise, it was not my father. A young man introduced himself as a reporter for one of the local newspapers. He showed his credentials and asked if she had a picture of my dad. When mother asked why he wanted a picture of her husband the reporter told her that the paper was doing a piece on citizens that had served in the war. They had received a list from the military and my father's name was one of those selected. My mother accepted this explanation and gave him the picture he requested.

The hour grew late, and mother grew more apprehensive. The guests began to leave. Soon it was just my grandmother and Grandpa Leo, who kept vigil with Mother. "Something is very wrong" Mother at last confided. "Pete would have called if he was going to be this late. I have a feeling that reporter was not being honest with me." Grandpa Leo tried his best to comfort Mother, but with little success.

Grandmother kept her eye on the window. Suddenly she spied a police squad car pulling up in front of the house. Two police officers got out of the car and headed for the door. "Eileen, the police are coming to the door."

Mother rose to her feet and made her way to the door. The officer's knuckles had hardly touched the door when Mother opened it. "Are you Eileen Lavery?" the officer asked in a terse manner. "Yes" mother answered, her voice just above a whisper. "Your husband was killed this afternoon in a natural gas explosion. You are ordered by the coroner to report to his office in the morning to identify the body." Having given their grim message, they turned and headed back to the squad car.

Mother didn't break down, she didn't cry, she just stood there in a state of shock. As Grandpa Leo led Mother into the house, Grandmother came running out, billfold in hand. Grandmother was a pioneer. She was one of the first women police officers on the Chicago Police Force. As those two officers made their way back to their car, they had no idea of the storm that was coming their way.

My Grandmother called out to the officers with her billfold open to show her badge. "Do you have a family, officer?" Grandmother asked the officer who had delivered the news. The officer nodded. She then asked the second officer the same question. The second officer nodded his response to the inquiry.

Grandmother stood in silence for a moment. She said nothing but simply stood seething in a silent rage.

In years to come, I would learn firsthand the bone numbing effects of my grandmother's silent seething pauses.

"God forbid but if one of you were to fall in the line of duty and the wretched assignment of taking the news to your wife fell upon me, is that how you would want me to do it? The least you could have done was to remove your hats and give a simple word of sympathy. You should have stayed to make sure the lady was alright. What would have happened had she been alone and passed out? She has a little girl who just turned one today. She also has a baby on the way."

Both officers stood in silence, heads bowed in shame. Grandma had so much more she could have said but she felt her place was with my mother.

Grandma had no idea if her words had made any impact on the young officers, but one thing was sure, she had given them something to chew on.

Mother's world had taken an unexpected turn. This morning, she had a husband, a future. Now she was a widow with a one-year-old child and another on the way.

For months to come my mother would look out the window every night waiting for my father to come up the walk. He never did.

In those days of darkness, the only thing that brought my mother any joy was my sister, Kathy, and the knowledge that a baby was on the way.

My sister and I had become by mother's world. We were her reason to go on. Her children would be the hope of her future.

CHAPTER 2

MY SISSY'S SMILE

It is written in the scriptures that God will never put more upon us than we are able to bear. Never has this scripture been more put to the test, and found to be so perfectly true, as in my mother's life.

As the time of my coming drew ever nearer Mother became more apprehensive. It was not the fear of yet another mouth to feed nor was it the thought of raising two children without a husband. Mother remembered all too well the extreme difficulty she had suffered only eighteen months earlier. When bringing my sister into the world, mother had suffered horribly. She struggled with hard labor for almost twenty-four hours. Today, there is no doubt, my sister would have been delivered by Cesarian Section. However, in nineteen fifty-four Cesarian Section was a relatively new procedure and was performed as a last resort. The birth of my sister was such an ordeal that the announcement of my coming was met with an "Oh no, not again," from my father. He remembered the last delivery all too well.

The apprehension that my mother felt, as the day of my arrival loomed ever near, could only be countered by my sister's wild excitement. Mother had gotten my sister on board with the idea of a new baby coming. Mother told Kathy about the new baby and asked her to help care for the new bundle of joy. This put my sister over the moon. The very thought of helping to care for the new baby made Kathy wild with excitement.

As Mother entered her final month, my sister would inquire on a daily basis if the baby was coming today. Mother would simply answer "soon" and that would suffice until tomorrow.

The day I was born started out as any other day. Mother prepared breakfast for herself and Kathy. As she reached up for something on the upper shelf of the cabinet, her water broke. Mother knew full well that the dreaded contractions were soon to follow.

Mother called Grandmother and Grandpa Leo first. Grandmother was off that day and Grandpa Leo had a car. Mother then informed Kathy that her dream was about to come true. Mother then took her to a neighbor who had offered to care for her when the blessed event came to pass.

Mother had already packed a bag in anticipation of the event. By the time Grandmother and Grandpa Leo arrived Mother was at the door, bag in hand. "How far apart are your contractions?" Grandmother questioned. "About five minutes," was Mother's reply as she got into the backseat. Mother patted Grandpa Leo on the shoulder reassuringly. "Don't worry Leo, we have plenty of time." I was born early in the morning which put poor Grandpa Leo in the middle of Chicago rush hour traffic. They were not far from the house when Mother began to groan. "Are you alright, Eileen?" Grandmother inquired. "No" came my mother's short, to the point, response. "The baby is pushing hard, and the contractions are coming faster." "I'm timing your next contraction" Grandmother announced. So, when my mother finished her contraction, Grandmother began timing. "Another one is coming now," Mother announced in a half shout.

A look of panic crossed Grandmother's face. "Your contractions are only two and a half minutes apart." I thought you said they were five minutes apart, Eileen." "Well, they were when we left the house, they were five minutes apart" Mother shouted. "How can that be?" Grandmother mused. "We haven't been on the road that long." "I don't know, Ma. Why don't you ask the baby." Poor Grandpa Leo, he made the mistake of chuckling. "Shut-up and step on it, Leo" Grandmother ordered. However, it was the height of rush hour and there was only so much poor Grandpa Leo could do.

Grandmother began calling out to some of her fellow officers. She would name an officer who worked the district through which they were passing. "Where is he at" she would mutter. After listening to this for several minutes, mother answered from the backseat, "I don't know, Ma. Maybe they are doing something silly like fighting crime or something." Suddenly, Mother felt Grandmother's hand on hers. "Eileen, why don't you just have the baby in the backseat." At this suggestion, my mother became very animated. "Ma, are you insane? There is no way I'm having my baby in the backseat of a moving car." Suddenly, Grandpa Leo chimed in, "We are almost there." To which Grandmother, in her quiet retiring way answered "Shut up and drive, Leo."

Grandpa Leo made it to the hospital and no sooner stopped the car when Grandmother jumped out and ran into the hospital to get help. In less than a minute a wheelchair pushing orderly was taking Mother to delivery.

Grandmother and Grandpa Leo headed for the waiting room. They settled in for what they thought would be a considerable length of time.

Upon her arrival in the delivery room, Mother was placed on the delivery table and awaited the nurse.

The nurse was a pleasant woman. She entered the room greeting my mother with a warm broad smile. "Let's see what we have here" she said cheerfully. Mother always laughed when she related how quickly the nurse's smile disappeared. The nurse picked up a phone and called for an intern, stat!

"I called my doctor before we came" Mother offered.

The nurse shook her head and smiled. "Honey, he will never make it. This baby is coming right now."

The intern entered the room just as my mother was preparing to push. "One push was all it took." Mother remembered. "You flew out like you were sitting on an ejection seat. The intern caught you in his breadbasket, with a grunt. You let out a very healthy scream and you were here."

Now back in the day, when a woman bore a child, she would spend several days in the hospital. For your first baby, it was a five-day stay. For all subsequent babies, barring complications, it was three-days. The babies were not left in the room with their mothers, as they are today. The babies were cared for in the hospital nursery. The babies would be brought to their mothers by a nurse, for short intervals, to bond. The majority of the time, the babies were in the nursery.

On the day Mother was discharged from the hospital she was handed the swaddled bundle, wheeled to the door, and wished the best of luck. She was now on her own.

It is at this point I must tell you, my sister talked to me and introduced herself to me before I was ever born.

Mother related to me that often in the night her sleep was disturbed by my constant movement. She thought very little of this, attributing it to my sleep patterns. However, one night shortly before I was born, mother found herself unable to sleep. After Dad died, Mother would often find her thoughts in the night would be of him. She lay awake, her eyes closed. She was big as a house and very uncomfortable. As she lay in the dark silent room, to her surprise, the silence was broken by a still small voice. "Hello baby! I'm Kathy, your sister. I love you." At this point mother felt me move around in her womb. I heard my sister's voice and positioned myself to better hear her. It was then that mother realized why I moved about in the night so often. My sister was talking to me. She told me of all the fun we would have, and she asked me to come soon. That night Mother realized just how close a relationship my sister and I would enjoy.

Grandma picked us up at the hospital. When the car pulled up to the house, Mother looked up to see my sister jumping up and down. As Mother entered the door Kathy greeted her with great joy and then put on a gymnastics show. Grandpa Leo had taught her some tricks and Kathy showed off every single one. Mother applauded from the couch and then asked if Kathy would like to meet her baby brother. My sister ran over and climbed up on the couch beside Mother. Mother very carefully pulled the blanket back from my face. Kathy sat for a moment in silent awe. I was sound asleep, my eyes closed tight. At last, my sister came close and whispered "Hello baby Michael. I'm Kathy, your sister. I love you!" Mother said that upon hearing my sister's voice, my eyes opened wide. I looked at her and my face broke into an ear-to-ear grin. Kathy looked at Mother and with an excited voice announced "Mommy, the baby is smiling at me, he likes me." Mother laughed "Of course he likes you, you're his sister."

From that time on I became the focal point of my sister's world. At the time of this writing, I am a man of sixty-eight years. Yet the sound of my Sissy's voice still brings a smile to my face and joy to my heart just as it did on our first meeting.

CHAPTER 3

MAMA WAS AN ANGEL

I suppose to the helpless infant, their mother takes on, as it were, a godlike status. This is by no means blasphemy but simply the truth. Of all the infants born into the natural world, the human is by far the frailest.

A newborn elephant is usually on its feet, taking its first unsteady steps within minutes of birth. On the other hand, depending on the rate of development, a human child can take between six to twelve months to take their first steps. The human infant is totally dependent upon it's mother for all of its needs. It is for this reason a bond exists from the womb.

We know our mother's heartbeat; we exult in her touch and the sound of her gentle voice brings with it peace and comfort. A father builds a relationship with a young child. However, for the mother, the bond is forged before birth itself. From the time the first sensations of movement are felt, a deep and abiding bond is forged. It is a bond which seemingly give mother's the endless patience required. The patience to meet every possible need the infant may require. They feed us when we are hungry. They change our stinky, disgusting poo poo diapers. They rock us to sleep and sit up all night with us when we are sick.

My mother was the center of my world. And my sister's world as well. Kathy did have the opportunity to get to know our father, if only for a year. I never knew him. I never felt his touch or heard his voice. I knew only Mother, Grandmother, Grandpa Leo and Kathy. Grandpa Leo would be gone before I was three years old, reducing my childhood sphere to only three people. The focus of my world was firmly placed on three figures, Mother, Grandma and Kathy.

As I began to mature from an infant to a toddler, my life took a turn. My Mother's image changed from that of the angelic provider of all things good to a Moses-like character who laid down the law set in stone. It is at this time in a child's life that their mother often is transformed from an angel to a meany. I too would have shared this view had it not been for my sweet Sissy.

Kathy and I were only a year and a half apart in age. Having already experienced this stage of life she was able to impart a great deal of toddler wisdom unto her younger sibling. Kathy could always speak to me in such a way so as to make me understand. I always understood her. Mind you, I did not always heed her sage advice. Much to my hurt I might add. However, in truth, I owe her a great debt of gratitude. During those terrible two years when children often become rebellious against the word NO my sister's sage counsel preserved me from more disciplinary action than I will ever know. Her gentle guiding hand helped me to understand that all of Mother's rules were for our good and well-being.

When I was a young child, the preschool movement had not yet come into its own. At the age of five a child was sent to kindergarten. Because my fifth birthday fell after school had already started, I had to wait until the following year to start my formal education. This meant I was nearly six years old when I started school.

While this knowledge was a source of some concern for my mother, I was more than happy to spend one more year as Mother's little shadow. Everywhere Mother went, I was right there at her side.

Back in the late fifties and early sixties, before the advent of the big chain supermarkets, the vast majority of people did their shopping at small, private family-owned shops. I followed Mother to the butcher shop, the small Certified grocery store, the corner drug store, the bakery and the small dime store. In every single case Mother was greeted by name and often with a hug. As a result of being Eileen's son, I was often the beneficiary of candy, cookies and even soda pop. It seemed to me that everyone in the whole world knew and loved my mother.

When we took the streetcar, many of the drivers greeted Mother by name. We would take a seat and without fail Mother would strike up a conversation with a stranger. However, it seemed to me nobody was a stranger. We would walk down the street and people driving by would honk and wave.

My Grandma was a police officer, so it was common for a squad car to pull over as we walked. The officer would lower his window and sing out "How ya doing, Eileen?" Even the law knew my mother.

Helping people was by no means uncommon to Mother. After our neighbor lost his wife, I can remember Mother, with me in tow, going over to visit with some food for him. She was beloved by nearly everyone in the neighborhood. What a glorious example she presented to a young, impressionable five-year-old boy. Service given from a pure heart. A heart that never sought anything in return.

I still remember when our neighbor passed away, Mother found out that he was being waked at a funeral home a few blocks from our home. We walked over and went in. It was early in the day, so no one was there. Mother sat me down in a chair and told me to stay there while she went up to pray for our neighbor. I watched Mother make her way up to the casket and kneel beside it on the kneeler. She bowed her head and prayed over a dear neighbor.

As I sat in the chair, watching Mother from across the room, I wondered. Is my mother an angel? To me, she looked angelic in the dim light. As a small, ignorant five-year-old boy, I concluded in my little simple mind that Mother must be an angel. I reasoned that only an angel could be loved so much, by so many.

CHAPTER 4

LIVING WITH THE LONE RANGER

As a child, I still recall with fondness the wonder of my favorite television shows. The one I looked forward to the most was the Lone Ranger. He was my hero. He and his faithful Indian Companion, Tonto fought the forces of evil to bring law and order to the old west.

I still recall sitting before the television with a cowboy hat and toy six gun ready for action. I sat on the edge of my seat waiting to hear the strains of the William Tell Overture. The narrator would sing out, "The Lone Ranger". I readily accepted his invitation, "to return to those thrilling days of yesteryear." For that half hour I was no longer a five-year-old kid, I was The Lone Ranger. I rode the range, righting wrongs, delivering the oppressed, punishing the guilty. When at last the episode came to an end, I must admit, I had a letdown feeling. I would have to wait an entire week to roam the plains once again with my good friend Tonto.

What I did not realize at that time was the simple fact that I lived with The Lone Ranger. At the end of World War II, my grandmother decided to take up a career in law enforcement. Up until that time, the work of a peace officer was strictly a man's world. But my grandmother was fearless and was unafraid to make a few waves.

Grandmother began her quest to become one of Chicago's first female peace officers, as a lowly crossing guard. One day while going through an old photo album, Grandma espied the old photo and showed it to me. There she stood, looking so smart in her crossing guard uniform complete with a large, handheld stop sign. She approached her crossing guard job with the same level of dedication with which she approached every job she had ever undertaken.

As I looked at the picture, my dear grandmother used this as an opportunity to teach me a valuable life lesson. Grandma tapped the photo with her index finger and smiled. "Michael, you must start at the bottom to get to the top". That sage advice has followed me all my days.

Once when I was interviewing for a job, the owner of the company, who would later become my good friend, Charlie, questioned me. He asked if I had any knowledge of the packaging industry. My answer was simply given in a single word, "No". He then asked if I had any experience working in a warehouse. Once again, my response was a single word, "No". Almost in a state of exasperation he asked if I had any forklift driving experience. Once again, I answered in the negative tense. It was obvious to me that the interview was not going well. I knew I had to say something, and fast. I informed Charlie that while it was true that I had no real experience in the warehouse field, I was a quick study and given the opportunity I would be running the warehouse in one month's time.

Wow! I had opened my mouth and could not go back. Charlie sat behind his desk a look of skepticism etched across his brow. "Do you really believe you can do that?" he rightly questioned. "I know I can" I answered in a most confident tone. Charlie's next question floored me. "If I hire you, will you show up for work?" I thought the question was rather silly, after all, what was the point of taking a job if you had no intention of showing up. However, after I began working, I realized why he asked me such a question.

Sir, you can contact any of my former employers and they will verify that my attendance was good. Charlie nodded and sat for a moment deep in thought. "If I hire you, how much would you want to start?"

"Six dollars per hour" I answered without so much as a moment's hesitation.

Charlie sat behind his desk for a moment in stoic silence. Fear gripped me. Had I overplayed my hand? Had I asked too much?

MAMA'S BOY:
A YOUNG BOY'S MEMORY OF CHILDHOOD

At last Charlie spoke, "Six dollars you say."

"Yes sir" I responded. Years later when we remembered that interview Charlie confided that he was rather shocked that I had asked so little.

My answer was simple. "To have asked for more, when I was totally inexperienced, would have been wrong. "You have to start at the bottom to get to the top." My Grandma taught me that.

Grandma went from crossing guard to meter maid. She did each job to the absolute best of her ability, without complaint or grumbling. From meter maid, Grandma went into officer training and ultimately became a policewoman.

Back in the late forties, women were not readily accepted by their male counterparts. This did not deter Grandma. In truth, it challenged her to prove that she was every bit their equal. She was a police officer.

When we lived on Nelson Street, we had a wonderful neighbor that lived two doors down from us. My Mother and Grandmother loved her dearly. She was a kind and gentle soul. She worked hard to raise her children. Her husband was not in good health and was of little help. She had it rough.

Her younger son had gotten caught up with a bad crowd. The young man himself was not a bad boy but he was running with bad boys. Grandma had several run ins with the young man. She warned him as an officer of the law and as his mother's friend to consider his friends. She told him if he continued on the course he was presently taking it would lead him to a place he did not want to be.

One-night Grandma had gotten home from work late. She got a call from our dear neighbor. As Grandma had predicted the young man had been arrested. Our neighbor was beside herself and asked if there was anything Grandma could do.

Despite being tired, Grandma got into her car and set out to help. Several hours later she returned with the young man and delivered him to his grateful mother.

I never knew what Grandma said to that young man. I often wished I could have been a fly on the wall. Whatever it was, it was memorable. From that point on the young man gave Grandma a very wide berth.

After we moved out of the neighborhood, Grandma would go back and visit our neighbor. Occasionally she would bring me along. On one such visit, we were surprised when the young son answered the door. His eyes lit up when he saw us. He told us his mother was out of town visiting relatives, but he invited us in. He asked if we would like something to drink. Grandma had some water, and I had a Coke. We sat in the living room and talked for a while. Grandma asked how things were going for the lad. The young man's eyes lit up. He told Grandma all about his new job that he loved. He also shared several other positive things that were happening in his life. I watched Grandma intently. She sat with an expression of great joy on her face.

When we rose to leave, the young man extended his hand to me, as the gentleman he was. Then he offered his hand to Grandma. She took his hand and pulled him to her and embraced him. She told him how proud she was of him. He in turn thanked her for what she said to him that night when she brought him home from juvenile hall.

That day Grandmother, who I dearly loved, grew in stature to me. To her ten-year-old grandson, she looked ten feet tall.

Not having a father had its drawbacks for a young boy. One day when I was in fourth grade I had an unfortunate altercation. I walked into the house and by the looks of me, it was easy to see who had gotten the short end of the stick. I was ill equipped to handle myself in a fight. Nobody had ever taught me the manly art of self-defense.

That night, as we sat around the dinner table, little was said about my altercation. My sister asked me if I knew the kid's name. I sat in silence, saying nothing. I couldn't tell my sister. If she went out and beat the guy up, I would be forever shamed.

When supper was over Grandma patted me on the shoulder, "Let's go downstairs." She spoke softly into my ear, hoping Mother would not hear. A feeling of dread filled me. What was downstairs? I obediently followed, with much fear and trepidation. What was about to happen I had no way of knowing. When Mother saw Grandma usher me out the backdoor, she asked, "Where are you going?"

"To the basement," Grandma replied.

"Why?" Mother inquired.

"The boy needs to learn how to fight. Pete's not here to do it, so I will." Grandma replied. Once in the basement, Grandma calmed my fears. "You're not in any trouble. I simply want to teach you how to defend yourself, so you won't get beat up again." I relaxed a little but was still scared.

"Make a fist," Grandma ordered. I couldn't make a fist. Grandma showed me how to make a fist so I wouldn't break my thumbs.

"I'm a bully, show me how you would defend yourself" Grandma barked. I began slapping wildly with my hands. Grandma shook her head. "We have a lot of work to do."

That night Grandma showed me how to make a fist and take a fighting stance. She taught me how to move my upper body up, down and backwards, how to block punches with my hands and forearms and not my head.

The next few nights Grandma taught me footwork off my fighting stance. In a week she had me dancing, bobbing and weaving. A professional prize fighter would have been impressed. The next week we focused on punching. Grandma showed me how to punch and move at the same time. By the middle of the week I was jabbing and punching, sticking and moving. I would stand in the middle of the basement and shadow box like a champ. By week's end, Grandma deemed me ready for my final exam. I came downstairs eager for my next lesson.

Grandma informed me that on this night we would fight with open fists.

"Take your fighting stance and let's begin." Grandma threw a punch, and I dropped my hands. Her open hand slapped my face rather hard. She looked at me in surprise.

"Why did you drop your hands? What's the matter with you?" I stood with tears running down my face.

"What's the matter with you? Fight!" Grandma shouted.

"I can't." I sobbed, shaking my head. "I can't hit you, you're my grandmother. I love you, my hand will stick up from the grave." A look of great tenderness crossed Grandma's face. But it did not last long. Soon it was replaced by a stern glare.

"Nonsense! You will stand and fight or I will slap you from one end of this basement to the other." Grandma moved in and the onslaught began. True to her word, the rights and lefts came in ever increasing volume. I began ducking and diving, bobbing and weaving. I block many blows with my hands and forearms. But no matter how hard I tried occasionally slaps would find the mark. Finally, Grandma dropped her hands.

"Look at me, Michael! I am not your grandmother. I am a bully intent upon hurting you. If you let me hurt you, I will go on to hurt someone else. I must be stopped, and you must stop me!" No matter how hard I tried, I could not envision my grandmother as a bully. The onslaught began again. I bobbed, I weaved, when suddenly a hard slap caught me flush on the cheek.

I don't really know what happened next. All I can say is that a breaker tripped off in my head. Before I knew what had happened, I threw a hard right that caught Grandma flush on the cheek. She staggered back into the highboy dresser. Grandma had a false upper plate. The force of the strike was such that her plate was halfway out of her mouth. She looked like a prize fighter languishing on the ropes. Her eyes were glazed; she shook her head from side to side trying to clear the cobwebs. I stood in stunned silence, my mouth agape. My eyes were as big as saucers, a look of pure terror on my face. They say people who have near death experiences often see their entire life flash before their eyes. I am here to tell you it is true. My whole life flashed before my eyes. I knew as soon as Grandma regained her senses, I was a dead man.

Grandma reached up and pushed her teeth back into her mouth. She then shook her head one last time to clear the last cobweb. Then she raised her gaze to me. I can't be sure but when her eyes met mine, I do believe my heart stopped for a moment.

Grandma straightened up and made her way toward me. I burst into tears. "I am so sorry, I didn't mean to hit you like that."

"Michael don't cry. You did nothing wrong." Grandma hugged me and kissed my head, and I knew all was well.

Then Grandma stepped back, placed her hands on my shoulders and looked me right in the eye. "That was good" she said smiling broadly. "That is one bully I guarantee will never be back. We both laughed, then she got serious.

"Michael, I taught you these things so that you could protect yourself. Never use what I have taught you to bully or terrorize anyone. Do you understand?" I nodded my head. "Because if I ever find out you did, I'll take you down here and show you what you don't know. Michael, fighting does not make you a man, but sometimes a man must fight. Do you understand this?" "I do." I answered. "Good, let's go upstairs and have a treat, I stopped at the bakery after work."

Grandma was getting older. She suffered from bouts of angina as well as arthritis in her knees.

After the riots that followed the death of Dr. Martin Luther King, Jr., and the Democratic National Convention in nineteen sixty-eight Grandma decided it was time to call it a career.

One Saturday night, while I was doing homework, Grandma approached me. She wondered if I would like to take a little ride with her. She didn't have to ask me twice. I needed a break. "Where are we going?" I asked, not really caring. Anything was better than homework. "Down to the station house, I need to return my service star. I am officially retired."

I couldn't help but hear her voice break. I could tell Grandma needed me for moral support that night.

Grandma's station house was located by the UIC Chicago Circle Campus. We pulled into the parking lot. She parked the car and hesitated for a moment. "Are you alright Grandma?" I asked softly. She looked over at me, a little smile crossed her lips and she nodded. We got out of the car and headed for the door. I opened the door for Grandma and had no sooner entered the building when a familiar voice rang out. "Is that my Cookie?" It was Grandma's old partner and my dear friend Helen.

Helen was very near retirement herself. She suffered from a very bad hip. Her days on the street were over and she was restricted to desk duty. "To what do we owe the pleasure Irene?" Helen asked. Grandma reached into her purse and pulled out her service star. "I've come to turn in my service star Helen." I saw tears welling up in Grandma's eyes and in Helen's eyes as well.

"So, you're going through with it Irene, you're going to retire?" Grandma nodded as she raised the star to her lips and kissed it. She then handed it to Helen. "Helen, will you make sure this gets into the hands of the right people?" "Don't you worry about it, Honey, I'll get it where it needs to go." Helen answered.

In truth I think apart from my Grandpa Leo, Helen was the only other person on earth that could call my Grandma Honey.

After Grandma had surrendered her badge, she and Helen began to share some precious memories of their days patrolling the streets of Chicago as partners. Though those days were far behind them, their recollections were as vivid as if they had been yesterday.

Suddenly, loud voices could be heard coming from down the hall. They were men's voices, and they were approaching us. Then about six uniformed officers appeared. One looked up and upon seeing my Grandma, and me standing at her side, let out a shout. "Look fellas, Irene is back, and she has a collar with her. Helen protested loudly. "That's no collar, that's my Cookie!" Helen always referred to me as her "Cookie", and I didn't mind at all.

The shifts were in the process of changing and these officers were coming off the streets. They made their way over and the officer who appeared to be the elder statesman spoke up. "So Irene, are you coming back to work?" Grandma shook her head and explained the job was for a younger person. The hall echoed with laughter. "You know that's right," many of the officer's agreed. Every one of the officers gave Grandma a hug and expressed the honor it had been to have served with her.

It was at this point that the elder statesmen of the group took my arm and pulled me aside. "Young man, they don't make cops like Helen and Irene anymore, they broke the mold. They're old school. Good cops, damn good cops. You should be very proud. Then he called out to Grandma, "Irene, the place won't be the same without you." With that, more hugs and kisses were passed around. Then it was time for us to take our leave.

As we made our way back to the car, I realized that Grandma had accomplished what she had set out to do. She had not only won the respect of her male counterparts, but she had won their admiration as well. She had served and protected the people of Chicago. She was a top shelf law enforcement officer.

Now, I'm a man, sixty-eight years of age and I still love the Lone Ranger. However, now I realize I didn't have to wait to return to those thrilling days of yesteryear as I did as a child. I lived with someone who stood for the right, championed the weak and helpless, and brought criminals to justice. I lived with a pioneer. My Grandma, Helen and their friend Alice endured the horse laughs and ridicule of their male counterparts. But in the end, they proved their mettle as top-of-the-line police officers.

No, I didn't have to wait for next week's episode, I lived with the Lone Ranger.

CHAPTER 5

THEN CAME JESUS

My Mother and Grandmother were by no means heathen. Yet my sister and I had never attended an organized church service. This was indeed a curiosity to me. From our home I could see the bell tower of a rather large church. Every hour I heard it chime and with each chime I wondered why we had never been there. Now, make no mistake, as a child, I probably knew just as much as most kids that attended Sunday School on a regular basis.

Mother owned an old Bible that she received when she had made her Confirmation. It was well suited for children. It contained many beautiful pictures. Mother told us all about Moses and the Ten Commandments. She even took my sister and me to see the movie. Wow! When I saw the Red Sea part on the silver screen, my five-year-old brain nearly exploded. What made the account even more fantastic was the fact that Mother told us it was not just a story. Moses was a real person. The Red Sea really parted, and Pharaoh's army really drowned.

Mother told us about Samson and his haircut that made him weak. She told us about David and Goliath. We knew about Daniel in the lion's den. We knew who Jesus was. We knew Christmas was His birthday, he died on a cross and rose on Easter. Mother taught my sister and me these things, all with the pictures in her Bible. However, we still never went to church.

I suppose it was inevitable that at some point I should ask the question. "Mama, why don't we ever go to church?" It was then that my mother told me of my father's request. Father belonged to a church. In his youth he attended regularly. The denomination shall remain nameless, however, in all honesty, it could have been any denomination. Father had told Mother that she could raise the children in the church of her choosing, however, he was adamant that his children never be raised in the denomination that he had been raised in.

It was our misfortune that everywhere we moved, that specific denomination was the only game in town. Had Father been alive, I am sure that Mother may have attempted to change his mind. But he was not alive. Consequently, Mother felt obligated to honor his wishes.

Many years would pass before Mother would tell me the truth behind my father's religious aversion. As a young man, I had always chalked it up to the effects of war. War had a way of doing that to many men. They went in as believers then the multiplied horrors of war took their toll. Many men returned admitting they had lost their faith. I was sure this was my father's unfortunate circumstance. But, as a young man, Mother related to me the true story.

My Father had been raised in church. In his youth, he never missed a Sunday. Adulthood did result in a slight fall off in attendance; however, he still did attend church. Then the war came. At war's end, my father returned to the life of a civilian. He found work, began to date my mother and settled into as normal a life as a veteran of that terrible war could.

War is a hellish experience. No one comes home unscathed. Father was no exception. Night terrors were a constant companion in the early years. Common sounds, such as a car backfiring would send him to the ground. Many G.I.'s turned to alcohol or drug use to ease their pain. However, many turned back to their faith. Solace was found in a church family. The faith of their childhood offered strength amid dark times.

After the war, Father began once again to attend church. One fateful night while coming home from work, he took a shortcut down an alley. While he did not realize it at time, this decision would forever alter his spiritual life. As he made his way down the darkened alley, he could hear garbage cans crashing and cats screaming. It was like one of those scary movies you would see at the show.

Suddenly, Father saw a solitary figure emerging from the darkness. The individual was very drunk and staggered into my father's path. The smell of the man's breath was itself intoxicating. The individual stumbled into my father. Father grabbed him, straightened him up, grasping him by the shoulders. As the man lifted his head to meet my father's gaze, he immediately recognized him. The recognition left my father cold. This man, who father had propped up beneath the dim streetlight was none other than his minister, for whom father had such great respect. Many things ran through father's mind at that moment. When he finally gathered himself enough to speak, all he could say was "Pastor, you're drunk". "Yes, I am." the minister snapped back. "But you tell us drunkenness is a sin" father protested.

The look that came across the minister's face was one of great indignation. He took his index finger and poked father's chest several times. "Now you listen to me." The minister bellowed. "You do as I say and not as I do, got it."

Father stood in disbelief, gazing into the face of a man he had respected. The minister straightened himself attempting to restore an air of dignity to his demeanor. "If you are quite finished, unhand me sir" he muttered. Father unhanded him and stepped aside. The clergyman continued his staggering walk down the alley.

Father would go on to marry my mother, father a child and have another on the way at the time of his death. Yet, in that time he never again darkened the door of the church. What horrors of war were unable to accomplish, one unfaithful testimony did.

Father was wrong to judge Christ by the moral failing of a man who claimed to be his minister. Always remember, men are frail and prone to failure. Always keep your eyes on the Savior who will never fail and does all things well. It is important to remember this no matter who you are dealing with.

People hold Christians to a higher standard. Spiritual failure can often have dire consequences in the lives of others.

Mother taught us many wonderful lessons by showing us pictures in her Bible. The difficulty was, my sister and I were entering a phase in our lives when new words would begin to dominate our vocabularies. Words like why, how come and what is that. When a child reaches this phase, pictures alone no longer suffice.

It was Christmas at our house, my favorite time of year. Of course, I would make my Christmas list as did my sister. We made our pilgrimage to visit the man in the red suit. We would present our requests and argue our case for sainthood. But to me, even as a child, there was so much more to Christmas than simply getting presents. There were Christmas parties. When I started school, I was most pleasantly surprised to discover we had Christmas parties at school.

Then there was the tree. Going to the tree lot with Mother to pick out the tree was always a momentous occasion. Putting up the tree, getting out the lights and ornaments, the tinsel as well as other decorations. Our house was transformed into a Christmas wonderland.

Everywhere you went, there were decorations. Then of course, who could forget all the holiday specials on television. A spirit of joy and goodwill permeated the air. Even a dumb five-year-old kid could feel it. But to be honest, the thing I loved best was the music of Christmas. I still love Christmas music. I think it's a pity that we only sing it once a year. Before the age of boring talk radio, Mother would keep the radio on during the holidays. Our house always echoed with the strains of heavenly Christmas music.

As I sit here writing, I must admit, my eyes tear up and I get a lump in my throat as I remember with joy the happiness that music brought to my five-year-old heart.

One December evening, we were sitting around the dinner table when Silent Night came on the radio. We all knew the song well, so we sang along. When the song ended Kathy asked a question, "What's a Savior?"

Now as I have stated before, my sister was, and still is brilliant. She was double promoted twice in the Chicago Public School system. She went from first grade to third, and from third to fifth grade. However, Mother said no to the second promotion. She did not want Kathy in high school at the age of ten.

Kathy asked questions. Not dumb kid questions like me, but intelligent ones. When Mother would answer, Kathy would put her finger to her lips and would process the information. It was like looking at a human computer. I am almost certain that at times her left eye would twitch. After Kathy processed the information, she would ask more questions. She was in no wise being obnoxious, she honestly wanted to know.

If I looked at a turtle and asked Mother a question, "Mama, why does a turtle have a shell?" "It is like a little house the turtle goes into when he is scared" she would answer. I would say "Okay" and skip off to do something else.

Not my Sissy. Oh no, she would process that information and ask ten more questions. My poor Mother. Kathy was the only person I knew who could make her sweat. To Mother's credit, she knew Kathy deserved answers. So, one day, when a man came to our door selling encyclopedias, Mother bought a whole set. Back before the internet an encyclopedia was as close as you could get.

Whenever my sister would start asking questions about anything Mother would simply say "let's look it up." We would look it up and Mother would read about whatever my sister wanted to know. I too would sit and listen intently. I learned so much from those encyclopedias. We all did. What a great investment. I still have them and occasionally look things up. Of course, they are very outdated, and the pages are yellowing. After all, it is the nineteen fifty-nine edition. Yet, I will keep them and will always cherish them. They are a tangible reminder of Mother's love for my sister and me. That set was expensive for that time however, Mother willingly made the sacrifice that her children might have every advantage to learn. That was Mother.

Well, getting back to my Christmas story, Kathy asked a question, "What's a Savior?" We both looked at Mother.

"A Savior is a person who saves you from something." My sister's finger went to her lips again. She was processing. "Do you mean, like if someone is drowning and a person pulls them from the water?"

"Yes," Mother answered. "The person who pulls them out of the water would be their savior." My sister's finger went to her lips yet again. "So, Jesus saves us from drowning?" Kathy questioned. Once again, we looked at Mother. Her head dropped.

"Yes, I suppose Jesus would save a person from drowning but that is not what the song is talking about. Jesus came to be Savior of the whole world. He came to save us from our sins." Now I knew what sin was. Sin was when a person broke one of the ten commandments. We knew what the ten commandments were. Mother had shown us a picture of Moses with the tablets in his hands. We also saw the movie with Charlton Heston as Moses.

While I was thinking about the chariots in the Red Sea, there stood my sister, index finger to her lips, processing.

Out of the blue Kathy asked, "Who is Jesus' daddy?" Mother answered without a moment's hesitation, "God is the Father of Jesus."

"So, Joseph is God?" Kathy questioned.

Poor Mother looked so confused. "No, Joseph was Mary's husband, Joseph was a carpenter."

"But if Joseph was Mary's husband that would make him the daddy of Jesus."

I looked at Mother, she was starting to sweat. She was out in some deep water. No picture in her Bible was going to bail her out of this one. Mother was in a spot.

In Mother's defense, I feel I must say a word here. I have been a pastor for forty-five years now. The incarnation of Jesus is the biggest stumbling block to many church going people. The incarnation of Jesus is a pillar on which our faith stands. Jesus, the Son of God, born of a virgin, died on the cross, rose from the dead on the third day.

I have talked to so many people over the years who have no trouble accepting the resurrection but when you ask them about the incarnation they shake their heads. It seems many people equate pregnancy with physical intimacy. Our concepts of God and His power have been skewed in our present age. People do not understand how God could have accomplished this. If you struggle with this concept, let me point you to Genesis, chapter one "And God said, let there be light and there was light." To place the living seed of His Son into the womb of a woman, took only a word. Let it be and it was. With God there is no such thing as impossible. However, I'm afraid explaining such things to a five-year-old and six-year-old would have been a real stretch. At last, Mother lifted her head. "Kathy, the birth of Jesus is a Christmas miracle from God." Kathy's index finger went back to her lips. "So, the birth of Jesus the Savior is a Christmas miracle." "Yes," Mother answered with a sigh. We may not fully understand it, but we believe it. "That is why it takes faith to believe in God. Because many things He does we just can't understand but we still believe."

Mother did a better job explaining those very difficult concepts than any theologian could possibly have done. However, it would be some time before we would take these spiritual concepts and turn them into tangible living realities in our lives.

As a little child I was so blessed. I had a Mother I thought was an angel. I had a grandmother who was a police officer. I had a brilliant sister who I loved dearly. I had good friends, a nice place to live and plenty of good food to eat. I was happy every night as I laid my head upon the pillow, feeling safe and secure. So, when Mother taught us to pray, it was a rather standard child's prayer. "Now I lay me down to sleep, I pray the Lord my soul to keep." Indeed, a very rudimentary prayer. Very simple, to the point, not all that taxing which is good for a little child's prayer.

I had no fears or distresses. As a little child I felt my parents were more than capable of protecting me from any danger. However, I remember one day when great fear gripped me, and I learned a valuable lesson about prayer and God's wonderful provision.

One morning we took Kathy to the corner of Sacramento and Belmont, where she crossed with the crossing guard on her way to school. As Mother and I headed home you could not help but notice the sky. It was very dark, and lightning began to flash across the sky. It was early April and rainstorms were by no means uncommon. This was very different. The wind began to blow, and the clouds looked much like water boiling in a pot. Mother took my hand, and we began a very fast walk toward home. We arrived home just as the rain began to fall. Mother ushered me into the house. I could not help but notice the look of concern on her face. I went into the dining room and sat at the table. Mother went into the kitchen and turned on the radio.

Several hours passed and the storm seemed to be getting worse. For the first time in my young life, I felt fear. "This is a tornado warning for this area. Be prepared to seek shelter on the lowest floor of your home, a basement or an inner hall."

Mother put me on her lap, and we listened together. "Mama, what's a tornado?" I asked. She thought for a moment. "A tornado is a spinning funnel of air that comes out of a cloud." She took one look at my face and knew I did not understand a single word she said.

"Michael, go get your pump top and a toy soldier." Mother knew I responded better to visual aids than long explanations. I brought my top and my toy soldier. Mother pointed, "Put your toy soldier there. Now pump your top and get it going really, really fast." I kept pumping the handle up and down until the top was really spinning. "Let it go." Mother ordered. I let go of the pump handle and the top began spinning wildly. It went to the right, then to the left, then straight. At last, it impacted the poor toy soldier. "That's what a tornado does, it spins very fast and when something is in its way, it moves it. Mother then said, "it's time for your nap, I'll take one with you."

I put my top and soldier away, then got into my bed. Mother climbed in beside me. "Mama, we don't have a basement or inner hall." "I know." Mother answered. "Maybe we should go get Kathy from school or call grandma and tell her to come home."

Mother put her finger under my chin and lifted my gaze to hers. "Michael don't be afraid. Kathy is safe where she is. The people at school know what to do. If there is any trouble Grandma will be needed to help people. We're safe here. God knows where we are." Mother's words comforted me greatly. Then she hugged me tight and prayed. "Dear Lord, watch over us now as we sleep. Protect Kathy and all the teachers and children at the school. Be with grandma at work. Be with all our friends and neighbors. Be with cousin Bill, Aunt Fran and Uncle Bill at work. In Jesus Name, Amen."

Though the lightning flashed, the thunder boomed, the wind blew wildly, and the rain pelted down, I slept sweetly. When I awakened, the sun shined brightly. Mother was in the kitchen making lunch. "Come have some lunch, we'll pick up your sister in a few hours."

"Look Mama, the sun is shining."

"Mother smiled, "Yes, it is, God takes good care of us."

I learned a truth, that is a reality to me to this day. God hears my prayers and is always good to me. That is not to say difficulty, fear or pain do not visit me as they visit all of us from time to time. However, I know, whatever storms of life may challenge me, God is greater than the storms. While I may be buffeted, I will never be consumed.

In nineteen sixty-one, I was six years old. I did not realize just how pivotal a year this would be in my life.

Grandma and Mother had decided that it was time to leave the neighborhood. The suburbs were blessed with newer and better schools. Grandma, being a police officer, knew our neighborhood was getting rougher. It was time to go. But the thought of leaving our neighborhood was most distressing to me.

I loved our house on Nelson Street. I thought it was the most beautiful house on earth. I had many friends in the neighborhood that I dearly loved. I didn't want to go to a place where nobody knew me. What about Helen and the other neighbors we loved so much? I thought about the kindly butcher and his family. Mother always bought her meat there. Nothing in that store was wrapped in plastic. She would order six pork chops or six chicken legs. If there were none in the meat case, the butcher or his son would cut your order. It never failed when we got home, Mother would open the package and find eight chops or legs. On our next visit to the butcher shop, Mother always came, money in hand to pay for the overage.

The butcher would laugh out loud. "Eileen, keep your money, that was my mistake. I was never good at math!" The butcher could count just fine. Back in the day, that was simply the way a shopkeeper showed their appreciation to their regular customers.

Then, of course, there was the elderly couple who owned the convenience store. They were so kind and always talked with Mother and treated us like family. On hot summer days they often gave us free pop. Such dear people, it's been six decades, and I remember them still.

How could I forget the Jewish bakery. The owner and master baker loved my mother. Every time we entered the bakery, the baker, his wife and the ladies behind the counter treated us like family had come to call.

Would we find such people in the suburbs? I thought not. But, of course, I was only six years old and had no real input.

Grandma and Mother had settled on a brand-new house being built in a place called Northlake. The house was across the street from my new school. When we made the move in September of nineteen sixty-two, the school across the street was only seven years old.

My new school was a big change from the school I attended in the city. The school in the city was old. My Mother attended the same school when she was a child. It was showing its age. The desks were bolted into the floor, and they had holes for ink wells. My new school was bright and clean with ultra-modern amenities for that time. I do believe that was one of mother's and grandma's main motivations for the move. It was all about my sister and I. Our parents wanted better educational opportunities for us.

So, like it or not, in early September of nineteen sixty-two we said goodbye to our house on Nelson Street, and we were off to Northlake.

We moved onto a block of bright new homes. My sister was in heaven, there were young girls everywhere. On the other hand, I was shocked to discover there were no boys my age. I felt somewhat like an orphan. I loved my new school, but school did not last all year.

The summers were lonely for me. To help alleviate this problem, my parents would invite my cousin Bill over to spend the summer. This was great because it gave me someone to play with.

Slowly, but surely, I began to settle into my new home. We had lived in Northlake about a year when, on a cool, dark fall day, the doorbell rang. Mother answered the door to a smartly dressed young man who told us of a church he had started in the area. Mother invited him in, and he told us of the new church he had started. The church was currently meeting in the high school. The high school is located behind our school. We could easily walk to church. Mother was very impressed with the young minister. He was thoughtful, articulate and well mannered. He handed mother his card and invited us to visit. Mother happily agreed to visit on Sunday. I was excited, we were going to church for the first time. When mother informed grandma of the young clergyman's visit, she too was very interested. She promised to go with us as soon as she had a Sunday off.

The next Sunday, mother, true to her word, had us up early. She fed us breakfast and dressed us up smartly. Then it was out the door and off the church. When we arrived, mother asked as to the denomination. She was careful to not break her promise to my father.

From my youth I always enjoyed listening to adults who were good public speakers. This young preacher had the gift. I sat on the edge of my seat. But, at a certain point in the service, all the young children were dismissed to Sunday School classes. I loved my Sunday School teacher. I loved the colorful flannel graph stories and the interaction with the other children.

On the walk home that afternoon, mother asked about Sunday School. Both Kathy and I gave a big thumbs up. We totally enjoyed the experience. Mother confided that she too had enjoyed the service, and we would be going back. This began our "Sunday go to meeting" experience. Grandma also liked the young minister and whenever she had a Sunday off, she went to church with us.

Over the years, mother and grandma's attendance slipped off. However, Kathy and I remained fairly regular in our attendance. When my sister entered seventh grade, she began taking confirmation classes. All young people who wished to be confirmed into the church were required to complete two years of confirmation classes. These classes usually took place during the seventh and eighth grades. Kathy, to her credit, made her confirmation while in eighth grade. She continued to attend the church while in high school. While in the church youth group, she met her future husband, Raymond.

When I reached seventh grade, I too began confirmation classes. Every Saturday morning it was off to church. I found the studies very interesting. I must tell you that I learned more about church history in my confirmation classes than I ever did in any of my college courses on the same subjects.

When I entered eighth grade, confirmation classes really took a turn. It was like Saturday School. We were given a thick textbook. We studied the history of our faith, from its roots in Judaism, to Loyola and the Jesuits, to Martin Luther and the Protestant Reformation. We had to read whole books of the Bible then write rather lengthy papers on a wide variety of subjects.

During this time, I noticed my sister and her boyfriend had stopped attending church. I thought they were of age and had decided to stop going to church. This was not the case. Kathy and Raymond had not quit church. They had started going to another church. I didn't know the name of the church or the denomination, but I did know something had happened to both of them. They went to church on Sunday morning, Sunday evening and Wednesday night. They were also involved in various church activities during the week.

To me this was mind blowing. I thought Saturday confirmation classes and Sunday morning church was kinda much.

Kathy and Raymond went to church five times a week. Not only did they go to church, but they really seemed to enjoy it. I liked going to church and confirmation class. I liked learning about God and church history. but I never really got excited about it.

God is a wise master builder. Albert Einstein once confessed that while he was not a religious man, he did know there was a God. When asked how he had come to this conclusion he simply pointed out that the universe was not the byproduct of a big bang. Instead, it was a product of an intelligent design, perfectly ordered, put into motion by a mind of unquestionable genius. A God that so intelligently designed the universe around us, in like manner orders the affairs of men. In each life he lays out the pathways that ultimately lead to a point of decision.

Little did I realize, as I made my way to confirmation class, that that God was laying out a path for me. The time of my confirmation was at hand. When at the end of one of our Saturday sessions, the Pastor gave us a most unusual assignment. He tasked each of us with attending another church a week from that Sunday. We were to take notes on the order of service. We were to consider some new ideas that might be incorporated into our worship service. I groaned inside. I didn't want to walk into some strange place where I didn't know anyone. I thought the assignment was very stupid. But an assignment was an assignment, so it was my responsibility to figure it out. By Tuesday of the following week, I was still perplexed. Where I would worship on Sunday was anyone's guess.

One day that week while I was unwinding after a day at school, Kathy came into the living room. She greeted me in a cheery manner. Upon returning her greeting it was obvious to me that something was on her mind. She sat down, she seemed uncomfortable and very tentative. This was unusual for my sister. Usually, she had no trouble in saying what was on her mind. In a somewhat hesitant voice, she finally spoke. Her question was something I never expected. "Mike, if you were to die today, would you go to heaven?" You could have knocked me over with a feather. While the bluntness of the question did set me back, the question itself offended me.

From the time I was very small, my sister was like a second mother. Kathy was always looking out for me. I understood the tenor of her question was not intended to make me look foolish. But to the contrary, was asked for my good. I sat contemplating her question for some time. To be perfectly honest, I had never really considered such a question. At last Kathy broke the silence. "Don't you know?"

"Well, of course I know. I most certainly would go to heaven; of this I have no doubt."

"On what do you base your answer?" Kathy questioned.

"I go to church every Sunday, I go to confirmation class, I am a good student. I'm nice to people and respectful to my neighbors. I am well liked."

My sister listened respectfully then shook her head. "Mike, you are all those things but I fear if that is what you have placed your trust in, heaven will not be your home."

"What do you mean?" I protested.

"Your good works are not good enough; you need Jesus as your Savior."

"I believe in Jesus." I retorted, doing my best not to let my aggravation show.

"I know." My sister answered. "But the Bible says Satan believes and we all know he isn't going to heaven.

"So now you're likening me to the devil?"

"Of course not," Kathy responded, "I'm relatively new at this. Come to church with Raymond and I this Sunday, they will make it clear."

"You want me to go to church with you this Sunday?" I asked.

"Yes, would you?" Kathy pleaded.

My dilemma was solved. I had another church to attend, and a ride to boot. "I'll be happy to with you." I answered.

"You can go with Ray and me on Sunday."

That Sunday I was up and ready. My sister and I waited for Raymond. Right on time Raymond pulled into the driveway. He greeted us warmly and we talked all the way to church. The moment I entered the building I realized this was not what I was used to. There was a sense of excitement. It reminded me of a sporting event. People were just waiting for something wonderful to happen. People were truly happy to be there. It was not fake or put on, it was genuine.

Never in my life had I seen people so excited to be in church. Kathy and Raymond took me around and introduced me to some folks. People shook my hand off and really made me feel welcome. Here I was, a thirteen-year-old boy who was being made to feel like a dignitary. Raymond took me up to the Pastor and introduced me. He shook my hand and talked to me like I was any old friend. But the most amazing thing to me was what had happened to Raymond.

Raymond was a great guy. I knew my sister wouldn't date a jerk. But to watch him shaking hands with people, laughing and talking really caught me by surprise. Raymond was shy. In the three years he had dated my sister, I was lucky to get a hello and good-bye from him. I had never seen him so animated and outgoing. I knew something had happened to him. What it was, I didn't know but it was significant, that I did know.

Now, when we broke up to go to Sunday School, I really had a shock. Sitting in the back row, were some fellas I went to school with. They were not friends of mine. Honestly, by the way they acted at school, I was surprised to see them at church. The Sunday School teacher was good. I could tell he had prepared the lesson well, but I found it difficult to pay attention. From the back row I could hear snickering and chuckles. I could hear whispers and knew they were talking about me. In all honesty, I don't think those fellas were talking about me. In truth I think they could not have cared less that I was even there. But when you are a self-conscious teenager in a new place, you think everyone is talking about you.

After Sunday School I met up with Kathy and Raymond. The church was so packed they had to open the overflow space. I couldn't sit with Kathy and Raymond because of the size of the crowd. I sat about four rows from the back on the main aisle. The guys from school sat on the last row. I just knew all their eyes were on me.

The church was beginning a revival meeting that day. The evangelist was named Patrick Henry. He was a descendant of the colonial patriot. After he was introduced, he stepped up to the pulpit and began his remarks with a joke. When he delivered the punchline, the entire congregation broke into laughter. I sat in stark horror. Uproarious laughter in the sanctuary? I braced myself for the lightning bolt I was sure would come. It never did, but to me laughter in the sanctuary was paramount to blasphemy. The sermon was unlike anything I had ever heard. The evangelist preached about the love of God. I had heard that many times before, but it did not stop there. He used many biblical passages and the Bible carrying congregation was encouraged to follow along. The evangelist spoke of the sacrifice of Christ and of the atonement that could only be obtained by faith. The works of men could not of themselves save. Only by faith in Christ could eternal salvation be obtained. Then he spoke of the judgement that awaited all those that rejected this truth. As the evangelist spoke of the judgements of hell, I trembled, just as Felix trembled at the preaching of the Apostle Paul. At one point during his message, the old evangelist looked directly into my eyes. I remember my blood ran cold. He pointed his finger right at me and spoke in a most ominous tone. "I bet you go to church every Sunday!" I sat in shock, how could he have known this? "You fancy yourself a very upright person with an above average intelligence." For a moment I relaxed thinking the evangelist was about to praise me. I was so very, very wrong.

"You probably feel if anyone deserves heaven it's you." A smile crossed my face. He must know me, I thought. Suddenly, without warning, he wailed in a loud voice "You are going to split hell wide open, you smug, self-righteous sinner." The words struck me like a bolt of lightning. Suddenly, I felt as if I were standing on a rocky ledge that was crumbly beneath my feet. I lowered my eyes to behold the turbulent, flame filled abyss. I sat in the pew sweating, my heart pounding. I was sure that I was within a hair's breadth of sweating blood.

I am aware that a great many people feel it is a terrible thing to ever go to church and be scared. However, hell is not just a mythical place, hell is very real. While it is not a popular topic, Jesus spoke more of hell than he did of heaven.

If you should ever question the validity of hell's existence, just consider the cross. Jesus Christ endured the cross to deliver Adam's fallen race from eternal judgement.

As I sat in a state of overwhelming dread, I was shocked back to reality by a voice I did not recognize. I looked up to see the Pastor of the church was now at the pulpit. He asked if anyone in the congregation felt they needed to invite Christ into their heart. If so, please raise your hand for prayer. I so desperately wanted to raise my hand but once again, my unfounded fear of what my fellow classmates might think hindered me. I could feel their eyes upon me and feared their ridicule. I feared something that was probably nothing more than a figment of my over-active imagination. Oh, what a fool I was to allow peer group pressure to discourage me from making the most important decision of my life.

As the invitation hymn began, I realized what I had to do. I stepped out into the aisle, but then stepped back. I did this three times. I cursed myself for my lack of resolve. I cursed my lack of courage when suddenly I felt a hand on my shoulder. I looked up, to see Raymond at my side. He had made his way to my side, but I had paid him no mind, so great was my anguish of spirit.

"Mike, would you like to go forward and receive Jesus?" He asked.

"Yes" I nodded in response.

"Well, why don't you go?" Raymond asked.

It was at this point I explained my dilemma.

"Tell you what, I'll go with you to the front, that way if they laugh at you, they can laugh at me too." With that, we were out of the pew heading down the aisle. Sometimes all a person needs is a little encouragement. I am so glad that when Raymond saw me struggling, he came alongside to encourage me to do the right thing. I will forever be grateful for the love and concern he showed me that day.

My Sunday School teacher led me to the Lord that day. There was no clap of thunder, the earth did not quake nor did the lights flash on and off. My salvation experience can be described as a sense of being lighter. I know that must sound silly to most who read this. However, it is true. I felt as if a very heavy weight had been lifted off my shoulders and now, I felt light as a feather. It was a sense of release and great freedom. I was baptized that same day as was Raymond.

For so many years I had been like the woman at the well. I worshipped a God I did not know. So many people fall into this category of worship. We recite creeds, we recite prayers, we worship God in an abstract sense. We believe in God, we believe that Jesus Christ is his son, we believe that he is Savior of the world. We believe in the work of the Holy Spirit in the world today. We study our religious heritage; we learn of the heroes of our faith. On a weekly basis we practice our faith. We believe so many things with our heads but never open our hearts to the Saviour who sacrificed himself for our sins.

For so many years I worshipped the God of my head. But on this day, the God, the Saviour who I knew with my head only became a living Spirit who I invited to live in my heart. Dead knowledge became a living hope. That which was an abstract concept was now a living reality.

At the time of this writing, my sister Kathy and brother-in-law Raymond have just celebrated their fifty-first wedding anniversary. I have shared many wonderful memories with them over the years, but none will ever surpass that day. When Raymond came up beside a frightened thirteen-year-old kid and was so instrumental in helping him make a life changing decision. I'll never forget it. Kathy, Raymond, I have nothing but love for you.

CHAPTER 6

OPERATION: BRING OUR PARENTS TO JESUS

The very name of this chapter seems to allude to a massive military operation. What I did not realize on my way home from church that day, that glorious day, was the reality of the situation. A struggle, a battle, was about to ensue. It would last for four long years. What I had originally thought would be so easy became a long hard life or death engagement.

I felt so wonderful, we all did, the day I got saved and baptized. All the way home we felt the excitement and thrill of the day. We talked and laughed; our hearts were filled with expectations for the future. I could hardly wait to tell Mom and Grandma the wonderful news.

As I entered the house my mother greeted me as always then the inevitable question was asked. "How was church this morning?"

I was as excited as a child on Christmas morning. "Church was great; I got saved and baptized today."

Mother broke into laughter "Oh no! Not you too." Her response was one for which I was totally unprepared. I looked over at grandma who just sat in stoic silence. Usually, my parents were very supportive of any decision that took initiative on my part. What other decision on the face of the earth could have possibly taken more initiative than this one, I thought.

Mother spoke up. "I hope you don't think this decision of yours is going to get you out of making your confirmation." Mother's reaction gave me a glimmer of hope. My decision did not anger her or grandma. They simply wondered if my decision was a well-crafted ploy to get me out of my confirmation. I assured them that I had no such intention. Actually, I had originally decided to go to church with Kathy and Raymond to fulfill a confirmation class assignment. Mother looked at me with skepticism in her eyes.

"Alright." she muttered. "Just remember you are finishing your confirmation classes and you are making your confirmation. Got that!"

"Yes, I do." I promise I will finish what I started. In truth, I rather enjoyed confirmation class. I looked forward to making my confirmation. I worked too hard for two long years. I sacrificed my Saturday mornings. Would I now just quit and walk away empty handed? Not in this life. Besides, I liked and respected the Pastor who taught our class. I often went to class half an hour early just to talk with him. The Pastor also liked and respected me. Once he told me that I had wisdom and insights that were far beyond my years.

I left home early the following Saturday morning. I wanted to see what kind of mood the Pastor was in. I feared my report might be somewhat controversial. There was one thing that was certain however, this week's confirmation class would be epic.

The good Pastor asked how many of us had completed the assignment. I believe we had six students in our class. It was fifty-four years ago so my memory is a bit fuzzy. However, I was the only person to raise their hand. The Pastor was visibly upset and after giving us a mild tongue lashing, he asked me to present my report.

As I have already mentioned, I had the greatest respect for the Pastor. He was a man in his mid-sixties and did not relate well to teenagers. I was somewhat fearful to present my work. I had so many suggestions; I feared my recommendations would not be well received. But, I was asked to present my report along with its recommendations and that is exactly what I intended to do.

I made such suggestions as the use of more scripture in the sermon. I also suggested the use of humor, strategically placed, of course. Parishioners should be encouraged to bring their Bibles from home to follow along. I encouraged the Pastor to have an altar call at the end of service. The Pastor took notes and asked many good questions. He did not seem angry or in the least bit upset. My fellow students who very often sat in silence chimed in with a multitude of good questions. I must admit, it was a rather spirited hour. It was my first opportunity to share my new faith and share it, I did.

When I arrived at home, as always, my mother asked how confirmation class went. She was always interested in how my school days went, how church went on Sunday morning and how confirmation class went. Often, I would simply shrug my shoulders and sigh, "okay". This would aggravate mother to no end. She was truly interested to know what was happening in my world. But, on this day, when she asked, I told her. I shared everything that happened. Mother did not find the story I related amusing.

"How could you show such disrespect for a man who has been in public ministry longer than you have been alive? Michael, do you think you have any right whatsoever to instruct him?"

I was dumbfounded. "Mother, the Pastor instructed us to write down differences in the service and make recommendations. Everything I did was well within the parameters of the assignment."

The next morning, during the service, the good Pastor implemented several of my humble suggestions. This action increased the respect I already had for the man.

A realization began to come over me. The conversion of my mother and grandma would not be an easy victory. They were not enemies of our newfound faith. They did not hinder our church attendance. They simply did not want it.

As I have said, in my youth, I thought my mother was an angel. She was always a fine woman who cared for others. She was loved and well respected even in our neighborhood. Grandma was a police officer whose whole life was to serve and protect the people of Chicago. They were moral and religious and felt they were more than able to stand on their own merit.

Kathy and I never gave up trying to win them despite an uphill battle. We witnessed to our parents whenever the opportunity availed itself. But we were mindful to not overdo it. It is often easy to witness to loved ones so aggressively that you turn them against the message. We were careful not to let this happen. There was another problem which in truth was more serious. Kathy and Raymond had surrendered their lives to full-time Christian service. As for me, while not as dedicated, I still attended church at least twice a week. Our philosophies and mind sets differed so greatly from those of our contemporaries that mother and grandma feared we were being brainwashed.

As I have mentioned several times before, my sister was brilliant. She knew mother and grandma's fears had to be addressed. Being her old, logical self, she realized the only person qualified to do this was the Pastor himself. Kathy presented her case to our parents. It was my opinion that she would crash and burn. Mother and grandma would never agree to a face to face with the man they believed brainwashed us all. But, my sister, like a seventeen-year-old Clarence Darrow presented her case. Much to my surprise she did it! Mother and grandma both agreed, a meeting would clear the air.

As the time of the meeting drew near, I was filled with dread. At times, grandma could exhibit an ill temper. I prayed the meeting would go well and would not be a reenactment of the night of the long knives.

The night of the meeting, all was in readiness. The doorbell rang. Kathy went down to answer it. Moments later she emerged leading the Pastor and a Deacon who accompanied him into the house. Introductions were made and the meeting commenced. Mother and grandmother laid out their concerns. The Pastor listened intently, nodding his head several times. After grandma had finished voicing her concerns the Pastor began his response by expressing his heartfelt appreciation for their concerns. He then went on to address every point in great detail. During the discussion a little levity was even shared. They laughed and talked, and I thought this is of itself a true miracle of God. No effort was made on his part to sidestep or skirt any issue. This greatly impressed grandma.

"That young Pastor addressed us like intelligent women." she confided to me years later.

After the Pastor had answered all our parent's concerns, he flawlessly shifted the subject to eternal things. He gave a masterful presentation of the plan of salvation. I sat in awe of his mastery of scripture and smooth as silk delivery.

Mother and grandma were attentive to every word. I was certain victory was at hand. Yet, when the Pastor invited them to receive Christ, they both said "No."

After some small talk the Pastor and Deacon excused themselves, and that was that. My heart sank like the Titanic. I was so sure of victory, only to see it slip away.

The summer of seventy-one was one of great change for our family. Kathy graduated from high school in June. She and Raymond were married in July. That fall, Raymond and Kathy moved to Pontiac, Michigan to begin Bible college.

I had started attending church with Kathy and Raymond about a year earlier. After I made my confirmation, I decided to go to the church where I got saved. I thought it offered greater opportunity for spiritual growth. However, I would be a liar if I said it was a no brainer for me. As I have mentioned before, I had great respect for the Pastor of my other church. I also had many people there who were special to me. Some of the Sunday School teachers I had known since the earliest days meeting at the high school. It was hard to leave them.

My sophomore year of high school, nineteen seventy-one seventy-two, was probably the most monumental year of my life. That was the year God called me to pastoral work. My life was changed forever. I totally immersed myself in the work of the Lord and wanted to be a part of every ministry. I began teaching Sunday School, I became an Awana Club leader, I captained a Sunday School bus route. On Tuesday and Thursday nights I went on visitation and on Friday nights I was involved in our Teen Club. Some of my high school friends came to know the Lord. For a Christian, there is no better feeling than to know God has used you to bring someone to himself. Yet, for all of this, I suffered with the knowledge my parents were not saved. I led others to Christ, but I could not lead my parents to saving faith. They were two very good people who didn't think they needed it.

God provides for us all the good things we need, and God knew I needed a mentor. It was at this time that God led a man into my life who was destined to become my best friend and mentor. Mr. Ken Vance grew up in the mountains of West Virginia. He grew up in a tough, hard, scrabble world. He was a young man when he went to work in the coal mines. The coal mines turned a boy into a man in short order. Mr. Vance told me stories of his younger days that made my hair curl. He would often tell me how God had interceded many times to spare his life. When he, at last, trusted Christ he felt such a debt of gratitude; he wanted to share the truth with everyone he had ever known.

Mr. Vance was the perfect mentor for a green, wet behind the ears teenage boy that wanted to serve Christ. We teamed up as visitation partners. I knew very little about evangelism. On the other hand, Mr. Vance was a master. I followed along and kept my mouth shut and my eyes open. He was a wonderfully personable fellow. When we were invited into someone's home he would converse on a wide range of topics. Mr. Vance had such a huge library of life experience that he had no problem finding things in common with people. I was always amazed at how comfortable he was at conversing with men and women alike.

I learned something during that time that would transform my future ministry. Before you can win a person to Christ you must win them to you. No matter what the topic of conversation would be, Mr. Vance was a master at bringing it back to the gospel.

It was on one such occasion that Mr. Vance skillfully brought the conversation back to the gospel. He turned to me and proclaimed, "This young man will now share the scripture with you." I must admit I was dumbfounded at first. However, I quickly recovered and shared the Romans Road. After I had finished my presentation Mr. Vance invited the folks to receive Christ. They did with great joy. On the way back to the car Mr. Vance slapped me on the back and exclaimed "Mike, God sure did use you tonight." In truth, I did very little, but Mr. Vance made me feel ten feet tall.

My parents had often seen Mr. Vance when he had come to pick me up for church activities, but they had never really met him. They asked me to bring him over to the house one night. This was the Lord's work. I knew if my parents met him, they would like him. If any man could win my parents to Christ, it was Mr. Vance. I told Mr. Vance of my parents' desire to meet him. He was happy to accommodate. We set the time for Thursday night and prayed for the success of our venture. Thursday came and we headed for my house. I was confident this would be the night. We arrived and my parents were gracious as always. I made the introductions and from that point on, it was like an old home week. To see Mr. Vance with my parents, one would think they had known each other from childhood. They talked and laughed like old friends. Grandma talked about her days on the police force, mother spoke of her harrowing experiences working on the broach and Mr. Vance spoke of his days in the coal mines of West Virginia. I sat spellbound and so encouraged. This would be the night my parents came to Christ.

As always, Mr. Vance seamlessly shifted the conversation to spiritual things. My parents were engaged, they asked good questions which Mr. Vance answered like the master he was. When the moment of truth came, however, both my parents said, "Not tonight, we want to think about it." The conversation continued a while longer and then we excused ourselves. My heart sank down to my feet. Mr. Vance could see I needed some encouragement, so we went to our favorite fast-food place and talked over coffee and Coke. Mr. Vance told me how much he enjoyed visiting my parents and what fine people they are. Then he said something that floored me.

"Your mother and grandma are fine people and that is the problem. They are such fine people they really don't think they need a Saviour. You know, people like your parents are the hardest people to win."

"They are." I muttered.

"Yep, they sure are." Mr. Vance continued. "Take me, for example. I was a hard drinking, hard fighting former coal miner. I'd been in the Army and the Navy and was mean as a snake."

"You were?" I answered in disbelief.

"I sure was. No one had to twist my arm to convince me that I was a sinner, but your parents are different. They are good people and sometimes good people don't think they need what Christ offers."

"So, there is nothing more to be done?" I asked.

"I didn't say that. I just think it's time we stop talking and let God work. You have witnessed to your mother and grandma. Kathy and Raymond, the Pastor and now I have witnessed to your parents. I think the time has come to be still and let the Holy Spirit do his work."

Mr. Vance was right. More discourse would accomplish nothing. We had done our part, now be still and let God do his.

Later that same week we received a call from Raymond and Kathy. They were excited about school and reported on all the things that were happening. I always loved these phone calls. The excitement in their voices and the work of the Lord in their lives encouraged me so much. I shared with them the visit Mr. Vance and I had with mother and grandma. I also shared the advice Mr. Vance had given me. I would not verbally witness again to my parents, but I would witness with my life. It was in the Lord's hands to take the seeds sown and make them grow. Raymond and Kathy agreed with me. We prayed together and committed our parents to the Lord. Now we wait for the Lord to work. I had no way of knowing then how hard this was going to be.

Months passed; a year passed with no visible spiritual movements in our parents. I began to wonder if our parents were beyond redemption. One night, just before I was to start my senior year of high school I couldn't sleep. I remembered the words my mother had once shared with me. Shortly after my father's death she asked the Lord to let her live long enough to see her children grow up. Now, my sister was married with a new baby. In a year I would be going off to Bible college. The primary purpose for my mother's existence would be accomplished. My parents were no longer young. Grandma was retired, mother did a man's job and now had to commute into the city of Chicago for work. I walked into their rooms and watched them sleep. They both were starting to show their age. I cannot express in words the feelings of my heart that night. I could not imagine heaven without mother and grandma. I sat in the living room and prayed. Suddenly, I found myself sobbing uncontrollably, I was broken. As a dumb teenage boy, I did not realize at the time just how important being broken is. I would soon learn that it is when we are broken that God does his greatest work. Once again, months passed with no movement, but God was about to move in his mysterious way.

It was a dreary fall Sunday. As I did every Sunday, I went to church. When I returned home, I made a beeline to the back door. It was cold and damp and I wanted to get into the house. As I began to climb the stairs, I noticed the side door of the garage was ajar. I opened the side door slowly and peeked in. Much to my surprise, mother stood at the workbench. A look of anger was etched on her face. She was in her own world and did not hear me come in.

"Mother, are you alright?" I asked with a good measure of concern. Mother's eyes darted in my direction.

"Michael, you're home." She made her way to the door.

As we headed for the stairs I asked the obvious question. "What's happened?"

Mother stopped abruptly. "While you were at church, your Uncle Bill came by." My Uncle Bill was a good man, I loved him very much, however, he could be opinionated to a fault and mule headed stubborn. Grandma could also be opinionated to a fault and mule headed stubborn. When you put two people with these personality traits together, in certain situations a massive explosion can result. According to mother, this is exactly what had happened.

"He made Ma cry. I got so mad I just told him to go home. You know, when we were kids Ma sent us to church. We made our confirmation together. I still have a picture of Billy and me, our new Bibles in hand, standing with our Pastor! He's supposed to be a Christian. How can he talk to his mother like that?"

I let out a sigh and plopped down on the porch steps. "Is he a Christian, Ma? Is that your idea of what a Christian is? Making a confirmation, getting an award Bible, joining a religious denomination? Is that your concept? Mother, so many people have shared the good news of Jesus with you. Have you not heard a single word that was said? Salvation is not based upon what we think, what we call ourselves or how good we think we are. Salvation comes to us when we confess our sin to God and invite his Son to take up residence in our hearts. When we stand before God one day, God will not ask us if we've been a good Baptist. God is going to look upon the doorposts of our hearts. If he sees the blood of his Son, Jesus applied to those doorposts it will be counted to us for righteousness. It is not what we have done, but what Jesus has done for us that transforms us." As I looked into my mother's eyes, for the first time I could see a glimmer of understanding.

"What do I have to do again?"

"Pray to God, confessing your sins, then ask the Lord Jesus to come into your heart." I answered in hope.

Mother nodded, "I will do that tonight before I go to sleep."

I accepted that and went into the house. Then I realized, for all I knew, mother might not live until bedtime. So, I put my coat back on and, out the door I went. Once again, I could see that side door of the garage open. As I entered, once again mother stood at the workbench.

"You know, Mother, I don't think you should wait until bedtime. I think you should ask the Lord to save you right now."

"I did, I prayed twice, just to be sure I didn't forget anything."

I was so thrilled. I couldn't express my heart's joy at that moment. All I could say was thank you, Lord! You used a very negative altercation to produce a very positive outcome. My rejoicing was soon replaced by a simple truth. Mother was won, grandma was not. The victory would not be won until they both were saved.

I needed to talk to grandma today, but how? I needed to speak with her in private, one on one. I decided this could best be achieved by grandma giving me a ride to church tonight. I looked in the living room, to see grandma in her chair, looking as if she were scanning the horizon for a solitary figure.

"Mother told me about the altercation that you had with Uncle this morning.

Grandma turned her gaze toward me and sighed deeply. "You know your uncle and I know my son. He got angry over something trivial."

I sat in silence for a moment before I answered. "I'm sorry you were upset."

Grandma looked at me and smiled. "I know my son. I'll give him a few days to calm down then I'll talk to him, and we'll hash it out."

I nodded, then made my request. "Grandma, do you think you could give me a ride to church tonight?"

"Doesn't Mr. Vance usually take you to church? I hope everything is well with him."

I assured her it was, I just wanted to ride with her tonight.

"Will you need a ride home?" Grandma asked.

"No, Mr. Vance will bring me home, I just need a ride to church."

Grandma looked at me long and hard. I knew she could see through me.

"What time would you like to go?" she asked.

"After supper would be fine." I replied.

I got to work on my homework then prayed for a good outcome to this important journey.

After supper grandma pulled the car out of the garage. I said one final quick prayer, kissed mother goodbye, and went out to the car.

How should I approach this, I wondered. I wanted to be subtle but strong. As I pondered my next move I suddenly blurted out "Mother received Christ today!" I recoiled in horror. That is not how I wanted to start this conversation.

"I know." Grandma answered calmly.

Well, now at least the ice was broken, I waded in.

"Grandma fell silent. This was a concern to me, knowing the emotional trauma she endured that day.

"Michael, do you remember the old house on Belmont Avenue?"

"I sure do, we spent a lot of time there when I was small." Grandma grew up in that house. Her brother, my Great Uncle Jake, lived there until he died.

"When I was a child, there was a lot of vacant land and even farms in Chicago proper. One summer I happened to see a huge tent being erected in a vacant field. My curiosity was aroused. What was this tent all about?" I wondered. "Well, one warm evening I happened to see a huge crowd of people around the tent. I was curious so I made my way over. I was greeted by a friendly gentleman who told me that this was a tent revival sponsored by the Moody Bible Institute. I was a little nervous and thought about leaving but the music was wonderful and the people so friendly, I decided to stay. Then an old gentleman got up and preached a sermon that was unlike anything I had ever heard. My heart was so moved that night. The preacher encouraged those who never had, to ask Jesus into their hearts. I was too afraid to walk down the aisle. Then he asked those who were still in their seats, but wanted Jesus as their Saviour, to pray with him. He led us in a prayer that was identical to the prayer that your mother prayed today. Michael, I prayed that prayer that night. When the preacher asked all those who prayed to raise their hands, I raised mine. I trusted Jesus that night." She said with great confidence.

We arrived at church very early, so grandma parked in the lot. I sat dazed and confused as if hit by a round house right. When I had, at last, regained my senses I asked why she had not shared this with us. Grandma let out a sight.

"Michael, you can't be a cop as long as I was without it affecting you. You see a side of people that often goes unseen by most. Unfortunately, it is often a very unpleasant side. It has skewed me to a point and left me very distrusting. When I was a rookie cop one of my first assignments was with the Bunco Division."

"What is the "Bunco Division?" I asked.

"The Bunco Division apprehends people who separate fools from their money by dishonest means. I worked the State Street beat in downtown Chicago. I walked up and down State Street, and when I saw a con man plying his trade, I would warn him and tell him to move on. If he had not moved along by my next round I would bust him. I'm sorry to say, a great number of con men and women used religious enterprise as their cover. When I saw the intense loyalty you all had for the young minister, I must tell you, red flags did begin to spring up in my head. I feared that you all might be getting set-up. However, upon meeting the young minister when Kathy asked him over to the house, I must admit that I was impressed. Then he sat with us at Kathy and Raymond's wedding reception. I found him to be very genuine and an excellent conversationalist. But at first, I did have my doubts. I fear you must excuse me when the old cop instincts take over."

"Grandma, I can understand your doubts, but that still doesn't explain why you never told us about your decision."

"Michael, you have to understand, my father was Swiss and my mother was German. Faith to us was a very personal and private matter. I must confess that I admire the way you all defend your beliefs so eloquently. I also admire the way you share your faith. But I was just not raised that way."

I understood and accepted grandma's explanation. I kissed her and thanked her for the ride.

"Michael, I'm happy you have all chosen the path you have."

I smiled and nodded as she pulled away.

I had called Mr. Vance earlier, to tell him that I didn't need a ride to church. He met me at the door and asked if everything was alright. I smiled and said it could not be better and I would tell him everything after church.

The Pastor finished his sermon early that evening and asked if there were any testimonies. I raised my hand; knowing many of the church folks were praying for my parents. I told them of my mother's salvation and my grandma's confession. Everyone rejoiced greatly at God's answer to our prayers. After church Mr. Vance took me to our usual meeting place and, over a pop, I rehashed the entire story to him.

"How does it feel?" Mr. Vance asked.

"I'm happy and relieved to know my mother and grandma are believers." I must confess that I consider my contribution to the days events stumbling at best. I just happened to have been there when God did his great work. The truth is many people played a significant role in what happened that day. My dear sister, Kathy, was the first person to share Christ with our parents. It was my sister who got the Pastor to come to our house. Raymond played a part as well in his witness to our parents. Then, of course, there was the Pastor and my good friend Mr. Vance. Yet, despite our best efforts, it seemed when all was said and done, we were right back to square one. I think Mr. Vance's advice to simply be still and give God a chance to work was pivotal. Yet, for me, the turning point was that sleepless night when my spirit was broken. It is only in our brokenness that God shows forth his great strength. His strength is indeed made perfect in our weakness. God does not call us to win. We are called to stand and sound the trumpet. It is the Spirit of God that brings down the walls of Jericho. So, we may sing with the psalmist of old. "O give thanks unto the Lord, for he is good: for his mercy endureth forever. Psalm 107:1

CHAPTER 7

LIFE LESSONS

My grandma has been gone for twenty-three years. My mother left us twenty years ago. While they are no longer with us in a physical sense, there is not a day that goes by that I do not hear them. The life lessons they imparted have shaped my life. Long after they have gone, they live on in the life lessons they taught. After I leave this sod, they will continue to live. I have imparted them .to my daughter and to others. In turn, I hope my daughter will impart them to her children someday. The greatest of all gifts that can be imparted to another is the gift of the knowledge of eternal life.

The second greatest gift consists of the valuable life lessons a parent imparts to their children. These lessons will forever shape our lives, our character and our relationships. They will be the forge, the hammer and the anvil that molds us and form us into the people we become.

I suppose if I were to consider all the life lessons my parents taught me and wrote each and every one they could not be contained in a single book. But please rest easy, in this chapter I will only present five.

Lesson 1: Santa Never Gives You Everything You Want.

Christmas to me was always a time of year that was magical. Yes, as children we longed for a visit to Santa to share our Christmas lists. Then, of course, Christmas morning was awaited with great anticipation. But that was not all there was to Christmas.

It was the Christmas story, that first introduced me to Jesus. It was the glorious music that I love to this day. I wish they would play Christmas music all year round. If I had my way, I would sing Christmas carols in church all year.

Putting up the tree and decorating the house was always great fun. Christmas seemed to change people. This is something that I noticed, even as a very young child. People seemed happier and more pleasant. Smiles abounded and complete strangers would greet you with a heartfelt "Merry Christmas". If ever a person exhibited this spirit, it was my mother. I remember one cold December morning, before I was in school, we walked Kathy to the corner of Sacramento and Belmont. There the crossing guard was stationed to get the children across the intersection on their way to school. Mother always had a heart for crossing guards. She remembered that my grandma was once one. She admired the fact that whatever the weather, they were at their posts faithfully to protect the lives of the children.

When we arrived at the corner, Kathy would kiss us both then wait to be crossed. Upon reaching the other side, she would turn and wave and then disappear in the mass of children. Usually after Kathy had made a successful crossing, we would head for home. However, not on this day. I was cold and pulling on mother's coat.

"Let's go home, I'm cold." I protested in my most pathetic voice.

Mother scolded me. "Be still Michael, I'm waiting for the crossing guard to finish. I'm going to ask her to join us for a hot chocolate at the bakery."

Suddenly, I was warm. The bakery was like going to see Santa. When at last, the last child had been crossed mother asked the crossing guard if she was cold. She nodded, making a shivering motion.

"Well, come with us to our favorite bakery. It's only two blocks down Belmont Avenue. They make great hot chocolate. Come along, my treat!"

"I could use something warm" the young woman laughed.

I could hardly wait to get there. The bakery was owned by a Jewish family, and they made everyone that walked through the door feel welcome. As we entered, the little bell above the door heralded our arrival. The baker's wife and two young women greeted us warmly.

They knew my mother by name. I looked at the display window, it was so festive. A huge menorah stood in the center, beside it was a Christmas tree, colored lights were everywhere. The wonderful smell of fresh hot chocolate and baked goods filled the air. Suddenly from the kitchen a booming voice rang out.

"Eileen, is that you?" From the back emerged the baker himself. He was a portly man with a full salt and pepper beard. He wore the traditional yamilka or yamaka on his head, and his black apron was always dusted with flour.

As I sit here and pen these words I see him before me. I can say with some assurance that by now the baker is no longer with us yet in my mind his memory lives on still, remembered with great fondness and affection.

Mother introduced our friend, the crossing guard. The baker shook her hand and hugged my mother.

"Girls!" He sang out in the most joyous tones. "Get Michael a cookie, hot chocolate for everyone."

I felt like I was in Santa's workshop as one of the girls came from behind the counter, a tray of cookies in hand. Decisions, decisions, they all looked so good, and they were still warm. I wanted them all. After careful consideration I made my choice. I then sat down to eat my cookie and sip my hot chocolate. The kind, jolly baker gave mother and the crossing guard a cookie too. Then he reminded mother to take a cookie for Kathy. Kathy was never forgotten.

"The shop looks nice." Mother commented.

"Thank you, it makes me feel happy." The baker replied.

"I do have a question." Mother had a smile on her face as she began her inquiry. "You're a Jew, yet you have all these Christmas decorations." The baker broke into laughter.

"My Jewish friends wonder the same thing, Eileen. I have my menorah in the window, I love and celebrate Hanukkah but I also love and celebrate Christmas. You know Eileen, Jesus Christ was a good Jewish boy."

Mother nodded, "you are right as rain." She answered.

I did not know the baker's religious views, but I just can't help but wonder if our dear friend was a Messianic Jew. The answer to this question I will never know in this life. However, as for me, I shall contend that he was.

"How much do I owe you?" Mother asked as we prepared to go.

"The joy you have all brought me this day is compensation enough." The baker laughed. "Speaking of Christmas presents, wait here, Eileen." The baker disappeared into the back. When he reappeared, he had a large round parcel in his hand wrapped in burlap, still steaming. He placed it in a double bag and handed it to mother. "Merry Christmas, Eileen. I know you love Jewish rye bread. Enjoy and Merry Christmas to all your good family."

If there is one thing I miss about my early childhood, it is the pre-big box store experience. Mother shopped at a small, family owned, Certified grocery store. She bought our meat from a small family butcher shop. The butcher, like the baker, knew my mother by name. He was notorious for giving her more than she ordered. The grocer would float mother credit when things got tight, knowing he would receive full payment the next pay day.

One Christmas ritual I enjoyed was going to the Christmas tree lot to pick out a tree. We always had a real tree with ornaments, tinsel and those big, hot, Italian lights. No matter how hard my mother tried to keep the tree hydrated those hot lights dried it out. Mother grew tired of vacuuming needles well into May.

One day while shopping, we passed the hardware store on Belmont Avenue. There in the window were aluminum Christmas trees, a six-foot tree and a four-foot tree with an optional color wheel. The color wheel made the tree change colors and I thought that was really cool. So, we went in. The hardware store was also a family-owned business. The proprietor was a retired construction worker and plumber. He could fix anything so when people came in with questions, he knew just what they needed. We waited patiently until he had finished with his customers. Then he came over and asked how he might help us. Mother explained that she was interested in the six-foot tree in the front window with the color wheel.

The fellow sighed, "That's expensive."

"How expensive? Mother countered.

"The tree with the color wheel will run you thirteen dollars!"

Now you may laugh, that someone would say thirteen dollars was a lot of money but back in those days, when an average worker earned between $8,000 and $10,000 a year, thirteen dollars was expensive.

Mother answered, "I'll take both." Wow! I was excited. I could hardly wait to tell Kathy.

The proprietor went into the back room and brought out the box. He began to disassemble the tree, putting each branch into a paper sleeve. Mother asked if he had any trees in stock, to which he answered, the two in the window were his last two. Mother felt terrible that she had made so much work for him. The kind man laughed and said it was nothing. He then packed up the color wheel and offered us a ride home. Mother thanked him kindly and gave him a few extra dollars for his extra work. She assured him that she and her little man could carry the tree the three blocks to our house. I was only five years old, but I was a big five and mother and I had no trouble getting our new tree and color wheel home.

That night my Uncle Bill called to ask mother about something or other. She told him about the tree and the color wheel. He asked if there were any trees left. Mother told him only the four-foot tree was left. Uncle asked mother to buy the tree. He did not want the color wheel. Mother looked at the clock. "We better get going, the hardware store will be closing soon."

Kathy and grandma were doing something together so, once again, it was mother and I that headed to the hardware store. As we walked up, the old proprietor was just locking up.

Mother smiled when she saw the four-foot tree still in the window. "Sir, can you please save that tree for me? I'll be back in the morning to pick it up."

The man laughed. "I'll box it up for you now."

"I can't put you through all that work, especially when you probably have dinner waiting for you."

"No trouble." He replied. He opened the door and turned on the lights. We went in and watched as once again he went into the back and returned with the box. Then he went to work. Once he had it boxed up, he again offered us a ride home. Once again, mother insisted she and her little man were up to the job.

That Friday my uncle came over after work. He paid mother and took his tree home.

So I ask you, how many places would give you customer service like that today? Not a big box store. The small family-owned businesses of years gone by did not view their customers as statistics. Instead, they viewed them as good friends' worthy of their time. The personal touch was forever lost when the big box stores put family-owned businesses out of business.

Christmas would not be Christmas without a visit with Santa. Kathy and I made our lists and about two weeks before the big day we would go to visit with the big guy. Now every kid knew that the Santa's at the department stores were not the real Santa. After all, the Salvation Army had a Santa on every street corner. Every department store in town had a Santa. They could not all be the genuine article. As I saw it, mid-December was crunch time up at the North Pole. There was so much work to be done, Santa could not possibly get away. So, he had an organization of helpers who dressed like him and took notes. Through a series of elf operatives, the information was passed along to the big guy. Through Santa's organization the intricate network of spy elves and parents would rat out the bad children. A kid had to watch himself if he wanted to be on the nice list.

Well, the day came for Kathy and me to make our yearly trek to a small department store about six blocks away. We usually had very small lists. Each of us usually had one toy we really wanted. So, we told Santa what we wanted and whatever else we got was gravy. Kathy and I sat on Santa's lap and told him our heartfelt Christmas wish. Then came the inevitable question, "Have you been a good boy or girl?"

Now, when my sister answered, "Yes, Santa." She was telling the truth. My sister was the poster child for the good kid. Me, on the other hand, when I answered, "Yes, Santa." I didn't always feel totally honest. But I must have been good because every Christmas morning was magical.

Kathy and I were usually up early on Christmas morning. I searched among the treasures and found the gift I had asked for. I also found many gifts I had not asked for but was thrilled to have. During the course of the day, we would either visit Billy or Uncle Bill would bring the family to our house. Billy and I would compare notes and play with our new toys and have a ball. We ate a wonderful feast and by nightfall, after everyone had gone home, we would be tired.

It was during this time of decompression that mother would sit with us and ask the question. "So, did you have a nice Christmas?"

We always answered with a resounding "Yes." Kathy and I were always satisfied with what we received. It never really crossed our minds to complain about what we did not receive.

Mother and grandma always taught us to be thankful for what we have.

"Don't waste tears for what you don't have. Instead, thank the good Lord for what you do have. Always remember there are people who have nothing."

We were by no means rich, but we were well fed, well-loved and lived in a nice house. We were blessed and we knew it.

One Christmas was different. That year, as Christmas Day was winding down, mother came and sat down between us. She asked her usual question. "Did you have a nice Christmas?" Kathy and I gave our heart-felt affirmation. Then mother asked a strange question, "Did Santa give you everything you wanted?" We were somewhat taken aback by this question. But, since she asked, I answered, "No, I did not get everything on my Christmas list."

To this answer, mother simply chuckled, "Michael, don't you know, Santa never gives children everything they want?"

Blasphemy! This could not be true. What about all the Christmas specials and Christmas stories? They all state that good children get what they ask for. This revelation caused a circuit breaker to pop in my head. My six-year-old brain was nearing critical mass; it was too much to process all at once.

I countered in stammering tones, "What about the list, he checks it twice you know and don't forget the spy elves."

"They just tell Santa if you've been good. They don't tell Santa what to give you for Christmas. As far as the list in concerned, in all the stories I've ever read about Santa, a list in never mentioned." She then read <u>The Night Before Christmas</u> to us. (The Night Before Christmas, Clemente C. Moore, 1822)

Mother was right. Santa filled all the stockings, but no mention of a list appears. She put her arms around us and spoke slowly and clearly. This was her manner. Whenever she was telling us something she wanted us to remember.

"Santa knows that if he were to give you everything you wanted, you would grow up spoiled. You would grow up expecting everything and appreciating nothing. Santa doesn't give you everything you want he gives you what he knows you will really like."

As mother spoke, a light went on in my head. She was right. I could see that now. From that time forward, I never again questioned why I did not receive something for Christmas. If it was not under the tree, I figured I just didn't need it.

Today, as a minister and a Christian, I often tell people that God has answered every prayer I have ever prayed. Some people have called me a liar and others simply shake their heads in disbelief. But it is true. God has answered my every prayer but not always the way I have prayed them. You see, dear friend, God doesn't always give me what I want. God gives me what I need.

Lesson 2: Outward Appearance Can Be Deceiving

When I started school, I walked as I had always done, to the corners of Belmont and Sacramento. But there was one big difference. Instead of dropping Kathy off and going home with mother, now I went to school with Kathy.

Mother gave me strict instructions to wait on the school steps for Kathy, after school. I obeyed for the most part. Only once did I think I was big enough to walk to the corner alone. Boy, did I get yelled at for that.

"Your poor sister." Mother yelled. "She will think something has happened to you." You see, my sister was dismissed from class about ten minutes after I was. That is why I was instructed to wait for her. Sure enough, as we made our way back to the school, here comes Kathy crying her eyes out. She had a friend with her who was trying to comfort her. The little girl's face was horribly scarred. She was holding my sister's hand. When mother called out, and Kathy saw me with her, they both ran over. Kathy hugged me so tight I thought I might break. Then she stepped back and hit my arm.

"Michael, what did you do?" she yelled.

From a hug to a hit, it was the story of my life. I told Kathy I was trying to be a big boy.

"Well, big boy, you just about scared me to death." She yelled.

"I told you he'd show up." Her young friend chimed in.

"You sure did. Thank you for staying with me." Kathy said, giving her friend a big hug.

"Who is your friend?" Mother asked.

Kathy introduced us but I said nothing, my head bowed in shame. Boy, that sure didn't turn out the way I planned. I thought about it all the way home.

Kathy's friend said how nice it was to meet us, then turned and headed home.

That night, at the dinner table mother inquired about her friend.

"She's, my friend." Kathy answered. I think she is one of the nicest kids in the whole school.

"I noticed she has scars. Do you know how that happened?"

Kathy nodded, "She was attached by a dog when she was small."

"How horrible." Mother answered

"Yeah, she sure is ugly." I added.

Mother's eyes darted in my direction. "Michael Henry Lavery, how dare you say that beautiful young girl is ugly. I will have you know she is beautiful. She is beautiful on the inside where it counts. Let me tell you something Michael Henry Lavery, that young lady is beautiful, but I am having some doubts about you right now."

"Yeah, Michael." My sister scolded, "Why don't you grow up for once?"

That's exactly what I tried to do, I thought, but I said nothing. I knew anything I said now would just make matters worse.

"Does she have many friends at school?" Mother asked.

Tears welled up in Kathy's eyes, she shook her head. "I think I am her only friend. The other kids call her monster child. She cries an awful lot."

Mother put her arm around Kathy. "I'm proud of you. You invite that young lady over to play and for dinner." Then she looked at me. "As for you, shape up young man!"

"Yeah, shape up." Kathy chimed in.

The day of the play date and dinner finally arrived. The young lady was so nice and polite. I asked Kathy if I could play a board game with them. Mother made a nice supper. We ate and laughed, and I could tell the little girl really enjoyed herself.

The sun was setting when mother said it was time to take my new friend home. I say, my new friend, because by the end of the play date the young lady was my friend too.

When we reached her house, the girl's mother greeted us warmly and invited us in. While our new friend showed Kathy her room her mother expressed her gratitude to my mother. Her daughter had few friends and spent most of her time alone.

"Kathy is her only friend that I know of." Her mother confided. "She has had two plastic surgeries and is facing at least three more."

My mother stood and listened; she had a real gift for feeling someone else's pain. Perhaps it was due to the fact she had suffered more than her fair share in her young life.

I apologize for not using my sister's friend's name. However, I must confess that I cannot remember it, but I sure remember her. You know, she was so nice that it wasn't long until I hardly even noticed her scars. That's what happens when someone's real beauty shines through.

On our way home that night mother announced we were going to the corner drug store for a treat. The drug store had an old-fashioned soda fountain. Mother said we could order whatever we wanted. She was proud of my sister, yet that night I received a reward too.

MAMA'S BOY:
A YOUNG BOY'S MEMORY OF CHILDHOOD

I would witness my sister's kindness manifest many times during our childhood. To this day Kathy is a true example of caring. Both she and her husband, Raymond are two of the biggest hearted and kindest people that I know.

As I sat at the soda fountain enjoying my treat that night, little did I know that by summer, mother would ask me to befriend someone special.

This young man was despised for handicaps that were no fault of his own. The persecution that he endured, on a daily basis, often drove him to acts of aggression.

Back in the late fifties and early sixties summer meant one thing, kids were everywhere. The older kids rode their two-wheeler bikes while the smaller kids, like my sister and me, rode various pedal toys. The sidewalks of Nelson Street were transformed into kid highways. We rode and laughed and played. We never felt fear, it was an age of innocence.

One day while I was outside playing, my eyes caught a glimpse of a solitary figure. He rode an old, beat-up pedal tractor. I had seen him before. It seemed he wore the same overalls and dirty shirt every day. His nose was continually running. His voice was gruff and loud. The boy was slightly taller than me, but not by much. He rode over and did his best to join the mass of kid traffic. Suddenly, the happy sounds associated with our play changed. Shouts of anger and rage rang out. Kids kicked at the boy. Shouts of "get out of here, retard" rang out. I stood off to the side and looked on in total confusion. At six years old, I did not understand the violence of this response. The boy had done nothing wrong. He was not aggressive he made no threatening ovations to anyone. He simply tried to join in on the fun. For his efforts he was violently rebuffed. Much to my surprise, even some of the adults that were out looked at the boy with disdain.

As a child I was very emotional. My heart was so moved, I found myself on the verge of tears. Seeing this display of rage upon a child that had committed no offense. Seeing such vitriol displayed not only by kids but by adults too.

I looked up to see our neighbor, and dear friend Helen. Standing on her porch she called out "Cliff! Cliff! Come over here and sit with me on the porch."

Now I knew the boy's name, his name was Cliff. He rode over to Helen's house and pulled his tractor off the sidewalk. When he stood to his feet and walked toward the stairs, I could see Cliff was crippled. He walked with a distinctive hop. He slowly made his way up the stairs to the protective embrace of dear Helen. She invited him to sit with her. She gave him some pop and they talked.

I was just a dumb six-year-old kid. I didn't really understand what I had just witnessed. All I could understand was the wrongness of the entire situation. But the thing that stays with me is the voice of our dear neighbor, Helen. In Cliff's darkest hour, her kind voice bidding him to come. That was sixty-two years ago, and I can still hear Helen's call.

Having now served in gospel ministry for the past forty-four years, that clarion call still rings forth in my mind. The call goes forth to all the Cliff's of this world. The forgotten, the despised, the rejected of this world. The precious voice of Jesus bids us all to come unto him.

"Come unto me, all you that labor and are heavy laden, and I will give you rest. Take my yoke upon you and learn of me; for I am meek and lowly in heart: and ye shall find rest unto your souls. For my yoke is easy and my burden light." Matthew 11:28-30 KJV

During those glorious summer days, we played from morning until night. But even a six-year-old child needs some me time. It was during one of these me time moments that the sound of taunting laughter and pleading voices came to my ears. I walked down the narrow gangway, that ran between our house and that of our neighbors. Houses in the city were built so close together that it was said neighbors could reach out their windows and shake hands. I opened the front gate and proceeded onto our small front lawn hedged in by bushes. I could see the neighbor's son riding a fine twenty-six-inch ten-speed bike. With him was his buddy, who also rode a ten-speed bike. I would say the boys were seventh or eighth graders. They were riding in tight circles, showing off their advanced riding skills. I found myself in awe of these boys until I made out a child in the midst of the circle. I looked hard, and realized it was Cliff. He was pinned in. He covered his head with his arms and begged to be left alone. But the more he screamed the more his tormentors yelled and slapped him in the head.

I must tell mother I thought, she will make them stop. I ran toward the gate when suddenly I was stopped in my tracks by an unearthly scream. It was like nothing I had ever heard. It didn't sound like anything that could come from a child. It was almost primal in nature. What I witnessed horrified me. It was as if Cliff had morphed. You must remember, Cliff was a boy my age and was similar in size to myself. But, as I looked at Cliff, he seemed to have grown several inches before my eyes. His eyes were bloodshot red and the veins in his neck protruded. As one of the boys rode by, he slapped Cliff in the head. Cliff threw his right arm out straight. When the kid ran into Cliff's arm, Cliff didn't move. The older boy went sprawling off his bike. As the bike flew past, Cliff grabbed the frame and hoisted the bike over his head. The neighbor kid was stunned but then jumped up.

"Put my bike down, NOW!" he screamed. The other kid just rode off about ten feet and watched in total disbelief. At the sound of the commotion, the neighbor kid's father came out the front door.

"Put down the bike, son." The man asked in a soft tone.

"No!" Cliff replied in a tone that resembled a growl more than human speech.

"Put the bike down or I'll call the police." The father demanded.

Cliff took the bike and hurled it with all his might.

The father looked at Cliff, a sense of rage in his body language. He told his son to put his bike away and get into the house. He told his friend to get lost. He then told Cliff he was calling the police.

"I wouldn't do that if I were you." It was the voice of our neighbor, Helen. Cliff hopped over to her and hugged her tightly. Then from behind me I heard the familiar voice of my mother. She had been watching from the upstairs window.

"I'll call the police for our neighbor. My mother is on duty this morning. I'll request her and her partner, Helen."

My grandma had a reputation in our neighborhood. She was known for her fairness and for helping people in trouble or in need. She was a real hero to me, as was her partner. People also knew that when my grandma was on the case she did not stop until she had the whole truth and nothing but the truth. If you were in the wrong or even thought you were in the wrong, seeing grandma and Helen walking up to your door was paramount to having Godzilla sitting on your front lawn. It was just something you did not want. Our neighbor looked up at the window where my mother stood in silence before retreating back into his house.

I stood dumbfounded for some time. I watched our neighbor Helen comfort Cliff, and I felt a deep-seated sorrow for his plight. After all, Cliff was simply defending himself from two bullies. At the same time, I was filled with fear. This boy, slightly bigger than I, had just unseated a boy nearly twice his size and weight. What's more, he had accomplished this with a single straight arm. And, of course, there was the fact that he had lifted a twenty-six-inch bike over his head and hurled it with great force.

In my heart, I felt sympathy for poor Cliff. But he did frighten me. If a boy, slightly bigger than me, could do these things to someone twice his size he, no doubt, could rip a child his own size, limb from limb. I made up my mind. I would be kind to Cliff while at the same time I would give him a wide berth.

Several weeks had passed since this incident. I was getting ready for bed early one evening and this was strange for me. I was the consummate night owl. During the summer, I seldom went to bed of my own accord. However, this night was very different. I wanted to get plenty of sleep because my cousin Billy was coming over the next day. I loved it when Billy came to spend the day. Billy was well liked by the neighborhood kids, so I looked forward to a great day indeed. As I sat on my bed, lost in my thoughts, I was shocked back to reality by the voice of my mother.

"Michael, come sit by me." Mother patted the place on the sofa next to her. I sat beside her. My heart was filled with dread. Was Billy sick? Had I done something to anger mother or grandma? My feverish little brain raced.

"Are you excited about tomorrow?" This question quelled all my fears.

"I can hardly wait." I squealed with glee.

"So, you are looking forward to Billy coming over?"

"Yes!" I shouted. Then I began to tell her of all the great things I had planned for our day.

"That sounds wonderful!" Mother answered, in a tone that sounded equally as excited.

Then mother made a request that made my blood run cold.

"Michael, tomorrow while you are playing with Billy and the neighbor boys, if Cliff happens by, I want you to invite him to play."

I sat in stoic silence. Mother could tell by my facial expression that I was in no wise taken with her suggestion.

"What seems to be the problem? Don't you like Cliff?

The question made me feel a deep sense of shame.

"It's not that I don't like him, it's just the fact that he scares me.

"Cliff scares you? Why is that?"

I could not understand why mother would ask such a question.

"Don't you remember what he did to the boy next door? He and his buddy are big guys. They ride around on twenty-six-inch bikes and are nearly in high school. Cliff is not much older than me. He knocked that kid off his bike with his arm then he picked up the bike over his head and threw it."

"If I remember correctly, those two boys were bullying Cliff. Cliff was only defending himself."

"I know, but he was super-human, like the Hulk."

Mother sighed and shook her head. "Do you remember last Christmas when those two bullies threw your sister, head-first, into a snow drift?"

"I sure do, Kathy picked me up after school and we were coming to meet you. Those two big kids came out of nowhere and threw Kathy into the snow."

"What did you do?" Mother questioned.

"Well, I got mad and started kicking and punching. I used the book I had brought for Show and Tell like a club. I bit one of those guys on the leg and drew blood. I'm not sorry, either. They had it coming, they had no right to do that to Kathy. She didn't do anything to them."

"I know." Mother answered. "But I remember you put up quite a fight against boys twice your size."

"Well, I was really mad, they had it coming."

"Well, maybe Cliff was really mad because he had done nothing wrong. He did not deserve the treatment he received at the hands of those boys."

I had no answer. Mother was right. When those boys threw Kathy into the snow drift, I saw red, I had no fear, I just wanted to hurt them.

Mother, having addressed the source of my fear, could still see I was hesitant to comply with her request.

"What seems to be the matter, Michael?"

I sat in silence for a moment. A deep sense of shame filled me. I knew mother would not be pleased with what I was about to say.

"Cliff is different." I almost shouted the words. "He is not like the other boys he is very different."

Mother sat and just looked at me for what seemed an eternity. I sat looking at the floor.

"Michael, do you remember the lady that works for the elderly couple that own the corner store?"

Please forgive me as I take a moment to get just a little bit nostalgic.

The corner store is something that is all but forgotten today. Back in the day, before the advent of big box stores and supermarkets, it was the place to go. The corner store carried a wide variety of household necessities. Housewares, food, utensils, medicines, toys. It was a regular cornucopia of neat stuff. Most of these establishments were family owned. Regular customers were known by name. I am sure you have guessed that my mother was one of these people. Whenever we entered the store a little bell above the door would herald our arrival. "Eileen how are you?" the elderly couple would sing out upon seeing my mother. There was a young woman that had worked for the couple for a long time. She only had one hand. This was very odd to me.

Being only fifteen years removed from the second world war and only five years removed from Korea, it was not unusual to see men missing an arm, a leg, a hand. Some had prosthetics, some not. But this dear lady, her hand was different. She had one normal hand, but the other hand was only a stump with five fleshy growths.

"One day my inquisitive six-year-old mind got the better of me. "What happened to your hand?"

"That is none of your business." Mother scolded. "Tell the lady that you're sorry for asking such a question."

I bowed my head. "I'm sorry. I hope I didn't hurt your feelings."

"It's okay." The young lady answered. "You didn't hurt my feelings. To answer your question, I can only say that I was born with just one hand, the other hand never grew."

All the way home I walked in silence.

"Are you so quiet because you are ashamed of the thoughtless question you asked?" Mother's question let me know that she was still put out with my thoughtless disregard for someone else's feelings.

"I'm very sorry, I was not thinking." I answered in a very repentant tone. Unbeknownst to my mother, my six-year-old brain had just suffered a short-circuit. In all my life, I had never seen a baby born less than perfect. That day I received one of the many reality checks that would come in my life. Not all little babies are born perfect. Now, back to mother's original question concerning the lady at the corner store.

"Of course, I remember her. She was born with only one hand."

"That's right." Mother answered. "Do you like her?"

"Well, of course I do." My answer was somewhat irritable in tone.

"But Michael, she is different, is she not?" Mother's question hit me like a right cross to the side of my head. I had no answer, there was no answer.

Mother hammered home her point. "Cliff was born with his problem just like the lady was born with only one hand. In truth, we are all different. People come in different colors, they speak different languages, some have round eyes, some have slanted eyes, some people have different customs than ours. However, it is not what we see on the outside, but what comes from the heart that sets a person apart. Kindness, love, respect, goodness are languages that all people understand. Be kind to Cliff, be his friend and he will be kind and be a friend to you."

Wow! That was a lot for a six-year-old mind to digest, but I determined that I would let Cliff play. I promised I would let Cliff join us if he happened to come by.

Mother kissed my head and gave me a big hug then sent me off to bed. As I laid down to sleep, I had no way of knowing just how monumental that next day would be. What was about to happen would change me forever.

The next morning dawned partly cloudy but there was no rain in the forecast. I was up early anxiously awaiting my cousin Billy's arrival. At last, Uncle Bill came and dropped Billy off; we immediately grabbed some toys and out the door we went to play. It wasn't long before we were joined by other boys from the neighborhood. I had the nicest toys in town and the coolest, all the guys wanted to play with my stuff. There we were, playing and having a wonderful time when it happened. Coming from down the street came a familiar sound. It was the unmistakable squeak of Cliff's rusty old pedal tractor. To my shame, I hoped he would just pedal on by, but he didn't. I ignored Cliff hoping he would keep going but he didn't. He just sat there and watched us. Even as a child I felt shame for the feelings I harbored at that moment. Then it happened. Cliff spoke up, his voice was not gruff and demanding, but pleading.

"Can I play too?" Cliff asked slightly above a whisper.

I stood to my feet and faced Cliff. The boy I saw before me was not a wild-eyed hulk child, bent on death and destruction. I saw a little boy; a sad little boy who was so alone, without any friends. Now I don't know if it is possible for a child my age to have an epiphany, but I think I did that day. I saw someone, not through my eyes, but through the eyes of another. I saw Cliff that day through my mother's eyes and my heart was touched with compassion.

"Cliff, go, park your tractor by the gate and come and play with us." When I said this, Cliff's face lit up like a Christmas tree. I remember it still. When I recall it, tears come to my eyes.

"Oh, boy!" He cried as he went and parked his tractor. When he hopped back over, I introduced him to my cousin, Billy. I asked Billy to show Cliff how to use the tank.

"Sure thing, come on Cliff, let me show you." They had a ball, setting up targets and shooting them with the tank. I could not help but notice the three boys that had joined Billy and I. They had stopped playing and became very sullen. Finally, one of them spoke up.

"We don't want him here, make him leave."

I stood up and protested "Why? What has he done to you? These are my toys and I say he stays." This seemed to satisfy the boys for a while, but inevitably they protested again

"We don't want him here, make him go."

"No!" I retorted. At this my cousin Billy chimed in.

"Hey kid, leave Cliff alone, he's playing nice, what's your problem?"

This time our rebuke did not silence our playmates. Suddenly, a voice from above rang out. "Then go! My son and his cousin say Cliff stays, so he stays. If you don't like it, you can go."

Unbeknownst to us, mother had been standing by the front room window and had watched the whole thing. The neighbor boys got up and left. Billy and I played with Cliff all that day. Cliff helped put my toys away and he didn't break a single one. We rode all over the neighborhood, me on my Irish mail, Cliff on his tractor and Billy on my pedal station wagon, that he loved so much. Later, mother gave us homemade popsicles. We played until dinner time, but our friend Cliff didn't want to leave. I think Cliff thought he was having a dream; a dream he might never have again. It was then he asked, with a tone of fear in his voice.

"Can I come back and play tomorrow?"

"Sure!" I answered. "You can come back and play every day." Cliff's face, once again, lit up.

Cliff took me at my word. Every day that summer he came and played at my house. As for the other boys in the neighborhood? They came back. When they realized Cliff wasn't going anywhere, they learned how to play with him.

In nineteen sixty-two we moved out of the neighborhood. I have not laid eyes on my friend Cliff for sixty-two years. As you can see from the many pages he is still remembered with great fondness.

In Sunday School we learned a little song. It told us that Jesus loves all the children of world. Children of every race and nationality. I'll take that song one step further. Jesus loves the handicapped, the blind, the maimed, all those with special needs, he knows and loves them all.

Thank you, dearest mother for teaching Kathy and I that all people have value. Cliff, thank you for teaching a dumb six-year-old just how special a special person can be. Cliff, my prayer for you shall always be that you are kept in the precious Saviour's hands. Blessed by the presence of his Spirit both now and forever. Your friend always, Michael.

Lesson 3: Is That The Best You Can Do?

My sister, Kathy is brilliant. She has always been brilliant, as long as I can remember. While going to school in the old neighborhood, she was double promoted, not once, but twice. She was the living embodiment of a true scholastic champion. As for me, not so much. Everything my sister was, I was not. Kathy liked school. Whereas I looked upon it more as an encumbrance to my playtime.

My sister excelled while I struggled to read. In the early years of my schooling, I was rather indifferent. This proved a source of continual aggravation to my parents. Both understood that the work ethic forged early in life was often carried into adulthood. However, to their everlasting credit, they never compared me to my sister. I was never shamed nor questioned as to why I could not be like my sister. But my grades, or lack thereof, were always a source of concern.

I can remember vividly bringing home my report card one afternoon. Kathy brought hers home as well. Both of my parents were home, so we handed them over for inspection. They looked at my sister's first. I guess they needed a source of encouragement before they looked at mine. As usual, Kathy had straight A's. After giving her, her due praise, they turned their attention to mine. I had taken the liberty of taking a sneak peek at my report card before I got home. I was afraid my grades were less than stellar. I expected both of my parents to be rather put out. But much to my surprise, they looked at my report card and said nothing. Then grandma took my report card and turned it around so that the grades faced me. She spoke to me in a subdued tone.

"Michael, I have only one question for you. I want to know, is this the best you can do?"

I must admit, I was taken aback by the question. I just sat there with a dumb look on my face and my mouth open.

Grandma continued. "Michael, we do not expect you to get the same grades as your sister. However, what I do expect from you is that you always put forth your best effort. If your best is a C, that's alright, but it must always be your best. In everything you do, you owe it to yourself to do your very best. To do less than that is indeed a disappointment."

As I sat and listened, the words of my grandma tore into me. In truth, I wish she would have scolded me or slapped me. It would not have hurt half as much. In my heart I knew I had not put my best foot forward. My thoughts were interrupted by grandma's voice, once again, repeating the question.

"Michael, is this the best you can do?"

I could not even look up. I shook my head. "No, grandma, that is not the best I can do." Then grandma asked me another haunting question.

"Well, what do you intend to do about it?"

"I am going to do my best. I am going to work hard and give one hundred percent in everything I do!"

Grandma smiled. "That is all I ask Michael, always do your best, always give one hundred percent in all you do."

From that time forward I worked hard. I would never be my sister, but I could be the best me. The thought of being a disappointment to my parents was unacceptable. My grades began to rise; this made my parents happy indeed. When the next report card came home, my sister once again was the top of her class. My parents gave her the praise that was her due. Their attention then turned to me. I handed over my report card and sat in silence. Mother opened the report card and viewed my grades while grandma looked over her shoulder. Then, much to my relief, they both smiled.

"Boy, you didn't lie when you said you were going to work hard; these grades prove it." Both my parents then told me how proud they were of me. I had classmates who told me their parents paid them a dollar for every A they received. But, as far as my sister and I were concerned, the knowledge that we had made our parents proud was an ample reward.

I worked harder and was determined to do even better. Everything I did, I did with a one hundred percent desire to be the best.

I remember my freshman year of high school. I had decided to try out for the freshman basketball team. I had played on competitive teams before, but they were all part of a league. In a league, your parents pay for you to join. You are then assigned to a team, and you play. In a try out, you can be cut, so it differs greatly from a league. I suffered under no delusions. I understood going in that I would by no means be the star of the team. But it was my hope to at least make the roster. When I showed up for the first day of practice, I was shocked. About one hundred young men had shown up for the try outs. This was discouraging because I did not know if my ball skills would measure up. I was about to receive an even greater shock. Ball racks were rolled out. I think these were just for aesthetics. I suppose they served as a reminder of what we were trying out for.

The first four days of try outs we never laid hands on a basketball. Instead, we were subjected to torturous physical rigor. As I pen these words, the vey memory of those first four days makes my sixty-eight-year-old body ache.

I can remember being lined up on the end line. On the coach's whistle we had to run flat out to the quarter court line, touch the floor with the palm of our hand and run flat out back to the end line. Then we ran from the end line to center court and back again. Then to the tree quarter line. And then to the far end line and back again. All at flat out speed while the coach screamed at the top of his lungs, go faster.

To do this drill once was an achievement. To do it three or more times almost took super- human determination. Then while our chests were still heaving, they took us out onto the track. The coach set the scoreboard clock to fifteen minutes.

"Gentlemen, on my whistle, I want you to run, flat out around this track for fifteen minutes. Eight laps equal one mile, let's see what you have in the old tank."

My high-water mark was about one and a half miles. But halfway through the ordeal I was sure that I would die. Then, of course, came the granddaddy of all tortures. The infamous guarding drill.

The coach would bark out, "guarding positions." We assumed the position. One hand above our head the other below our waist, knees bent, upper body leaning slightly forward. To stand in this position for half a minute caused pain. What happened next made the Chinese water torture look like a Sunday School picnic.

"On my whistle, you will shuffle in the direction I point. Do you understand?"

"Yes, sir!" we shouted back. It was then that the torture began. The coach blew his whistle, pointing forward, backward, left and right. The cadence was slow at first but soon it got faster and faster. The coach's hands moved so fast that you had to pay close attention so as not to collide with someone.

After several minutes the shoulders, back and hips burned like fire. There were times I could not even feel my thighs. This resulted in some of the guys falling down. And when this happened, it often resulted in a chain reaction pile up.

The coach would yell "Get up, get up, keep going."

When, at last, the coach waved his arms, signifying the end of our ordeal, a loud collective sigh could be heard. The whole drill only lasted three or four minutes, but for those who survived, it seemed like an eternity.

"Are you having fun yet?" The coach would scream, a sadistic smile on his face.

After each trial, I would shower and go home. I would eat my dinner, do my homework and die.

On day one we had one hundred men or more. By day two, we had forty. By day four, we had twenty-six. On the fifth day the coach started out by making us run for fifteen minutes. After running our legs off, the coach ordered us to take a seat on the bleachers.

He looked around and then shouted. "Where is everybody?" Laughing, he pointed his finger at us. "You fellas are my survivors." Then he pointed at the ball racks. "Let's play some basketball and see what you got."

The freshman had two teams. The A team consisted of the best players. The B team were players who were not quite as good, but still could be whipped into shape. I was on the B team and not even a starter.

Now, as I said before, I did not labor under some grand delusion of greatness, but I did think I was better than the second string of the second team.

One night, I came home from practice and sat in sullen silence at the dinner table. This was not lost on my grandma.

"What seems to be the problem, Michael? You are unusually distant tonight."

The question caught me somewhat off guard. My first inclination was to say that I was tired. But before I could open my mouth to answer, grandma asked in her point blank manner.

"Didn't you make the team?"

This question made a perfect segway for me to lodge my complaint.

"Well, grandma, I did make the team."

"Isn't that wonderful. Congratulations, you worked hard and earned it."

I thanked grandma for her kind words, but then with a distinct tone of disgust, I continued. "Yes grandma, I made the second team, and not only that but the second string on the second team." I had no ill will toward any of the coaches. Inside I felt like a failure. I fully understood I probably would not make the first squad, but to be second string on the second team was for me most humiliating. "The coach made me the team manager."

"Sounds like an important job." Grandma answered.

"Oh yes, it is. I get to roll out the ball racks before practice. After practice, I collect all the balls and rack them up and put them back in the equipment room. I also get to collect all the dirty uniforms, tube socks and warm up jackets for both the A and B teams. I hamper them up and ship them to the laundry for cleaning. Come Monday, I fold them up; all nice and neat and place them in the freshman cabinet. I did not join the team to be a wash woman. I joined the team and worked, sweat and endured one hellish drill after another to play. They told me I made the team, but the truth is, I feel like I was dismissed."

"Well, what ya gonna do?" Grandma asked. Then she asked another question. "Ya gonna quit?"

"Quit? Quit?" I answered in disgust. It was rare indeed when I raised my voice to either mother or grandma. But, on this occasion, I did just that. "I'll have you know that when try outs began, we started with one hundred boys. They made us suffer they tortured us that first week. When the smoke cleared only twenty-six of us remained." Then I pounded my chest with my fist and shouted "I was one of those twenty-six. I won't quit, I'll be the team manager and a good one, too. But when I have finished my duties, I am going to practice with the team. I'll work to get better and who knows, maybe one day I will get my chance." Suddenly, I realized how loud I was talking and sat down. I looked at grandma. She just sat in silence and stared at me. Then I could see a glistening in her eyes. At last, she gathered herself and spoke.

"Michael, I think something has happened to you. I think you have left being a boy and have become a man. Real men never give up. They don't cry or pout. They work harder and try harder. Michael, you will learn that the greatest men and women in history succeeded because they did their best and soldiered on, even in the face of overwhelming difficulty."

Well, I must tell you that grandma's words spurred me on to study up on history. I think of the great English Admiral, Lord Nelson. Nelson was a sailor's sailor. His men loved and respected him. He demanded that every man under his command do his duty to the best of his ability. He was stern, but fair, leading by example. Nelson always led from the front. In the heat of battle, he could always be found on deck shouting orders and words of encouragement to his men. No man could ever question Nelson's courage. He lost his right eye and right arm to wounds suffered in battle.

I can imagine being a sailor aboard the English flag ship, Victory. Our fleet is small, it consists of only twenty-seven ships, sailing off the coast of Spain by the Cape of Trafalgar. Before us looms the combined fleets of Spain and France. Fear grips the men, when suddenly upon the quarter deck, an imposing figure emerges. He has a patch over his right eye, his right sleeve hangs limp and empty. He comes to the main deck, his one good eye fixed upon the enemy. With his left arm he motions for the battle flags to be raised up Victory's main mast. Nelson's message to the fleet was concise.

"England expects that every man will do his duty." England did not expect every man to be a hero. England expected every man to do his duty, to the very best of his ability. With that, Nelson's voice rang out in clarion call.

"Gentlemen, prepare to engage the enemy." Sharpshooters were often placed on platforms, high up the masts. In the midst of the battle, one such sharpshooter mortally wounded Nelson. Carried below decks, Nelson clung to life. Several hours of agony passed when a young officer came down the stairs. He knelt beside the dying Admiral. He spoke softly but clearly.

"Admiral Nelson, the French and Spanish fleets have fled, the day in ours."

Nelson looked up at his officers and smiled. "Thank God, I have done my duty." Those were his last words.

Nelson set the bar that his officers and men followed to a great victory.

Admiral Chester Nimitz was the Supreme Allied Commander for all US Naval Forces in the Pacific during the Second World War. After the bloody battle for Iwo Jima had concluded, Nimitz was asked in an interview to give his assessment of the battle. Nimitz sat in silence for a moment, his face was etched with emotion.

"Gentlemen, Iwo Jima was a place where uncommon valor was commonplace." Who were these warriors, for whom uncommon valor was commonplace? Were they Spartan warriors, trained from their youth in the art of war? Who were these men that faced off against an army of Samurai warriors who lived by the creed, death was to be preferred before dishonor? Who were these men? I'll tell you who they were. They were ordinary men who, when their nation called, they answered. They were the fella that worked at the corner market and loaded your groceries. The young man, who in his youth delivered your morning paper. The cop that walked the beat in your neighborhood. The milkman who delivered your milk and cream and butter every morning. The fella that worked in the machine shop down the street. They were ordinary Joe's who, when their country called stood up and did their best and won.

Later in life, as I served in ministry, I learned that even the scripture bore out this truth. Colossians 3:23 states: "And whatsoever ye do, do it heartily, as unto the Lord, and not unto men. God expects every Christian to engage every work of his hands with heartfelt vigor. Not for the praise of men, but for the glory of God. God expects no less that our very best effort.

I wonder if my grandma had any idea what the long-term ramifications of her simple question that day would be. "Michael, is that the best you can do?"

It still echoes in my mind and serves as a perpetual reminder to always do my best.

Lesson 4: A Real Man Never Strikes a Woman

I grew up in a home full of women. There was mother, and grandma and my sister, Kathy, even our dog, Peco, was a girl. So needless to say, from my youth, I was instructed in the way a gentleman was to treat the fairer sex.

When we rode on public transit, if all the seats were taken and a woman entered the bus, mother would have me rise and offer her my seat. Now, I must be honest, this did not always make me happy. But mother always said, "A real man never sits while a woman is standing." When entering a building my mother and sister would wait while I opened the door. Upon entering, they would thank me while I stood there and held the door for everyone that followed behind them. Mother always made it clear that good manners made young ladies feel special. I was so drilled in these things that they became second nature to me. To this day, I open doors for ladies and willingly give up my seat to ladies.

Now, as I made clear earlier in this book, I love my sister, dearly. She was like a second mother, she was a playmate in our youth, a friend and a confidant. We seldom ever had a cross word. But then, my sister became a teenager. Suddenly, she changed. She would bring girlfriends over to visit. I went from being a dear to a nuisance. Sweet, dear little Michael was now introduced as the "little brother". How I hated that term.

As I said before, my cousin Billy often came and spent the summer with us before Uncle Bill and the family moved to Northlake. It was during one of Billy's summer visits that I would learn a lesson that would forever stay with me.

We had only two bedrooms. Mother had one while Kathy and I shared the other. Kathy had one side of the room while Billy and I had bunkbeds on the other side. One day Billy and I were playing army on the floor of the bedroom. We had transformed the floor into a battlefield. American soldiers, with their Russian allies, were locked in a life-or-death struggle with soldiers of Germany and the Empire of Japan.

Into the midst of the carnage, my sister entered. She spoke in a lofty voice as if she were royalty.

"Michael, Billy my girlfriend is coming over to visit. You need to clean up this mess immediately." Now this did not make me happy, but I did realize it was, after all, her room too. Billy and I began to pick up the soldiers. Billy understood that I had a method of putting away my soldiers. When done correctly, they all fit into the box nicely. However, on this day my dear sister was not at all happy with our progress.

"Hurry up!" she demanded. "Come on, they're just dumb soldiers. Hurry it up."

My cousin and I picked up the pace, but it still did not do. Suddenly, Kathy began scooping up armfuls of soldiers and indiscriminately throwing them into the box. My dear cousin Billy, ever the diplomat, tried in vain to explain my system.

"Kathy, stop it." I protested, but to no avail. "Kathy, stop it." I shouted once again. When she refused to listen, she gave me no recourse. I slapped my dear sissy's face. I feel at this point; an explanation is in order. It was not much of a slap. The impact failed to so much as turn my sister's head. I would characterize it more as a biff or a smack. But my sister let out a scream. You would have thought I had struck her with a closed fist.

Her scream so startled Billy and I that we both jumped back. Kathy put her hand to her cheek.

"You slapped me! How dare you. I'm going to tell mother."

"Go ahead, you big baby. I hardly touched you." I retorted. My sister ran down to the basement apartment where my mother was with our tenants.

Billy stood with his face ashen, and his eyes fixed on me.

"If I were you, I would run." He advised

"Nonsense!" I answered. "I'll explain the whole thing to mother. I am sure she will see it my way." Hindsight being what it is, I should have listened to Billy.

Suddenly, from the front hall I heard what could best be described as a roar. "He did what?" was all I heard. Then I heard mother's pounding footsteps coming up the front stairs. The door opened and my mother and sister entered. As soon as my mother's eyes locked mine, I knew I was in big trouble.

"Mother, I can explain!"

"There is nothing to explain." Mother retorted as she removed her shoe from her foot. Before I could react, she grabbed my arm and began paddling my buttocks. Now before anyone cries child abuse, I must tell you about the shoe. The shoe was a house shoe. It consisted of a woven upper and a flimsy sponge rubber sole. Despite my mother's best efforts, I hardly felt it.

Mother had a habit of expounding the severity of my transgression as she doled out my punishment. She timed her words to correspond with each swat.

"A. Real. Man. Never. Strikes. A. Woman!"

"But Ma, she asked for it." I countered so weakly.

"I. Don't. Care. What. She. Did. A. Real. Man. Never. Strikes. A. Woman! Ever! Mother put her shoe back on her foot. Her face was red; she was breathing heavily. My spanking had taken more out of her than it had out of me. Yet, there I stood crying. Not because I was in pain but because I was ashamed.

My mother faced Billy. "I'll never forget the look on his face. I thought he was going to faint.

"Do you have something you would like to say?"

Billy shook his head wildly. "No, Aunt Eileen." He muttered.

Mother then turned her eyes back to me. "Is there anything you would like to say to your sister?"

I looked at Kathy. She just stood there looking sad. I thought she might be smug in her victory but that wasn't my sissy.

I walked over to her and without saying a word, leaned over and kissed the cheek I had smacked. "I'm sorry Kathy. I should not have slapped you."

A small smile crossed Kathy's face. She said nothing but simply smiled.

"Michael, I want you to always remember, a young lady is always to be defended and never abused."

The day I slapped my sister was the last time I ever raised my hand against a woman. Chivalry is not dead. To our shame it is no longer taught. I thank God I lived in a house where the true precepts of manhood were not only taught but expected.

Lesson 5: A Real Man Takes Responsibility for His Actions

One summer evening when I was a kid, I was playing with some friends in the backyard. My grandma came in from working an afternoon shift. Grandma looked so smart in her police uniform. It always made me so proud. She greeted all of us warmly and went in the back door. As she walked by, one of my friends made a comment.

"Boy, you sure are lucky to have a cop for a grandmother."

I quickly corrected him. "My grandma is not a cop. My grandma is a Chicago Police Officer." Now, unknown to us, my grandma had heard my little friend's comment. When she had entered the back door, she stood in the shadows. She listened so intently to our conversation.

"Cop, police officer, who cares? What really matters is the fact that you will never have to worry about getting into trouble."

His comment made me feel uneasy because I knew it was not true.

"I don't know about that." I answered sheepishly.

"I do. You have a get out of jail free card. You can do whatever you want. Your grandma will always bail you out."

This kid sure didn't know my grandma.

"I don't know." I answered. Then, as often happens when kids talk about such deep subjects, the conversation changed and as suddenly as it had begun, it ended. But the topic of our conversation had not been lost on grandma.

That evening, after supper, she retired to the living room. She took a seat on the sofa and called for me to come. She patted the place beside her and asked me to come and join her.

"Michael, come here and sit by me, I want to talk to you."

Usually when grandma wanted to talk to me, I knew I was in some kind of trouble. However, as my mind raced, I could not think of a single transgression. Then, the smile on grandma's face set my mind at ease.

"Michael, I just want you to know, in the event you should every get into trouble with the law…" As grandma spoke, my mind went back to my playmate. "I want you to know that if you are guilty of breaking the law, I cannot help you. Please, do not drop my name, for I fear you would cause me to lie by saying I did not know you." My jaw dropped. Grandma had just dropped a bombshell on me. If I ever broke the law, I would be on my own.

"Your mother and I have discussed this and are in agreement. We would let you sit in jail."

It took me a minute to get over my initial shock.

"Don't you and mother love me?" I questioned in a most pitiful tone. "Why would you let me sit in jail?"

Grandma did not hesitate to answer. "Michael, it is because we love you that we would not rush to remove you from your trouble. It is important that every young person comes to grips with a single reality of life. Actions carry with them certain consequences. Taking responsibility for one's actions is an integral part of becoming a real man. If we deliver you from every bad decision, you will go through life never learning anything. While it would be very hard for us, we would leave you to face the consequences of your actions. A lesson hard bought is best taught. Do you understand what I am saying?"

I nodded my head because I did understand. Someone who is always delivered from every foolish decision goes on to do the same things again and again. Even at the age of seven I could readily understand this concept. Grandma hugged me and kissed my head.

"Now, young man, you be careful to stay out of trouble."

"I sure will." I answered. And thanks to that heart-to-heart talk, I did.

That was my grandma. She was never one to mince words. She said whatever it was that was on her mind, whether you liked it or not.

It was mid-August of nineteen seventy-three. I was about to start my senior year of high school. The start of school was only two weeks off and I faced it with great anticipation. I was chomping at the bit to start Bible College. But before that was possible, I had to finish high school.

One morning, as I sat at the kitchen table, grandma joined me. She did not look good at all. She said she had suffered through a rough night and still did not feel well. She said she was going to try to make a doctor's appointment. Then she asked if I would drive her to the doctor's office, which, of course, I agreed to do.

Grandma did manage to arrange an early afternoon appointment. Our doctor's office was on Wolf Road and on this day, it was crowded. In front of the office there was not a parking space to be found. I had to double park, turn on my emergency flashers and help grandma up five stairs. Once I had her situated, I had to run down to the car and go find a place to park. At last, I parked the car two blocks away. I made my way back to find grandma still sitting where I had left her. There was a large crowd of young people waiting to get their school physicals. The majority of these young people were young women I went to school with. Many of them greeted me as I sat down beside grandma. I returned their greetings, and we exchanged some small talk as we waited our turn to see the doctor.

I must say, the young men and women that I attended school with were indeed a wonderful group of people. To this day, when I'm waxing nostalgic, I pull out my old year books. I see pictures and remember names and wonder whatever happened to some of my classmates. I still remember my high school years with great fondness.

When the doctor stepped out of his office door, he took one look at grandma and told her to come through. I helped grandma into the examination room, then went to wait in the outer office. I could hear the doctor talking to grandma. He lamented the fact that all these kids wait until the last minute to get their physicals.

"Irene, you have a virus. I'll give you a shot and a prescription. Take two pills a day and in three days you will be back to your old self."

"I sure hope not." Grandma answered, evoking a hearty laugh from the good doctor.

In a few minutes they emerged from the exam room.

"Take care, Irene. If you are not better in a week, call me."

The good doctor patted my shoulder, and extended the hope that he would not see me soon. I sat grandma down, gave a farewell wave to my classmates and headed out the door to get the car. I ran to where I had parked and drove up to the doctor's office. Once again, there were no parking spaces to be had. Again, I had to double park, turn on the flashers and run up to get grandma. I entered the waiting room and took grandma by the hand.

"Ready to go, grandma?" I asked with a smile across my lips. Grandma nodded and rose to her feet.

What happened next horrified me, and it would have horrified any teenage boy my age. Grandma turned to my classmates and said "It was so nice talking with you young ladies, bye now."

"Bye Mrs. Lavery, nice to meet you. Bye Mike, see you in a few weeks."

I smiled and waved, "see you in a few weeks."

Out the door and down to the car we went.

Grandma had talked with the young ladies I went to school with. The thought of this filled my heart with terror. This terror increased exponentially when I took my place behind the wheel. As I glanced over at grandma, she was looking at me in the same way that a cat looks at a bird. I found myself wanting to scream out loud. I didn't, I kept my cool. We went to the drug store and then home. I parked the car in the garage and shut it off.

"What did you say to my classmates? She still sat, with that little half smile plastered on her face. Finally, I said "What, grandma?"

She simply shook her head "I never knew you were such a lady's man."

"Grandma, all those ladies that you met today are friends of mine. We have been in study groups together. They are all smart and very nice. They all have boyfriends.

"I know that." She laughed. "But I must tell you, those young ladies are quite taken with you. When you left to get the car one of them asked if I was your mother. That was a nice compliment, I had no idea that I looked so young."

"Grandma." I protested.

"Well, I told them I was your grandma. Then they all began to tell me what a nice young man you are. One of the nicest in the school, I believe one of them said."

"Okay" I said, as I got out of the car. I helped grandma into the house, gave her one of her pills and made sure she was comfortable. As I turned to leave the room, I heard grandma call me.

"Michael, come sit with me and let's have a talk."

Reluctantly, I sat down opposite her.

"Michael, I know you have no girlfriends. I know those nice young ladies that I met today are just your friends from school. But I also know you will be off to college next year. We need to talk."

When grandma wanted to talk, you would be well advised to let her talk.

"Michael, I admire you greatly. You have goals, you have a plan, you know what you want to be, and have a laser focus. Most young people your age don't know what they want to study. You are a good man. You love God, Jesus is your life, and you live what you believe. With all the temptations and pitfalls that are out there for young people you have somehow managed to keep your nose clean and stayed out of trouble. I'm proud of you."

Grandma was never one to heap praise upon anyone. To hear her say such things to me was the earthly equivalent of hearing Jesus say, "Well done." I sat in silence for a moment, as if waiting for the other shoe to drop. When it did not, I answered grandma's praise with a simple truth.

"I had a lot of help."

Grandma nodded, "I know you did. That being said, I must warn you that even the most holy and dedicated of men have fallen to the temptations of the flesh. You can meet a girl in college, fall in love and fall into temptation before the wedding. You can fall into temptation on a date, with someone you do not love. In either case, it can result in a baby coming."

I knew she had a good point. I thought of David in the Bible. No man is above temptation. I knew the simple truth, no matter how strongly you may say such a thing could never happen to you, it most certainly could.

"Now, let me tell you what will happen if you ever get a young lady pregnant."

I felt myself breaking out in a cold sweat. I prayed that she would not produce her loaded service revolver.

"If you should ever get a young girl pregnant all those wonderful dreams, goals and ambitions are over. If you love the girl, then you will marry. If it is simply a question of two young people being stupid, I would not push you into marriage. However, in either scenario, a child is coming that must and will be cared for. Seeing as you are the father, you will get a job and support that child. He or she will know you as their daddy. You will bring them over here. They will know me as great-grandma and your mother as grandma."

At this point, she got very quiet. Her lips began to quiver. I could see she was becoming emotional.

"I have seen too much in my life. As a police officer, I have seen hundreds of small, helpless children abandoned. Left all alone in the most deplorable conditions."

Then grandma pounded her fist on the table beside her.

"Michael, no great-grandchild of mine will ever go through life with the question, who is my daddy?"

I thank God every day that I had a mother and grandmother that loved me so. Two women taught me the true meaning of manhood. A real man is not someone who has impregnated many women, and never raised a child. A real man is not someone who can beat the daylights out of any man who crosses his path. A real man appreciates what he has. He respects all people, giving no thought as to race or social standing. A real man has the courage to put his best foot forward and always does his best. A real man understands that a woman is precious, she is to be honored and always respected. Chivalry should be honorable and never considered less than manly. A real man always accepts responsibility for his actions. These are attributes that make a man, a man. These are the lessons my parents instilled in me.

You can say that times have changed. The definition of manhood has changed. But I contend that the definition has not changed. The problem is that young men today are not being taught these simple principles. Not only are young men not taught but they do not see these principles lived out before them by their fathers. The tragic truth is simple. How can we teach principles to the next generation that we have never been taught? We are seeing the fruits of a generation of young men that have not been mentored by their elders. So many children have never experienced the love of dedicated parents. How can they be expected to pass along what they themselves never received?

Thank you, mother, thank you, grandma for the wonderful lessons you taught my sister and myself. Thank you for a home where I always felt safe and loved. Thank you for punishments that were never dished out in rage but were always purposed to teach. Love was always the motivation, with the intent of keeping us on the right path. Know dearest mother and grandma, your children rise up and call you blessed.

CHAPTER 8

GONE, BUT NEVER FAR AWAY

My grandmother passed away in January of two thousand and one. My mother followed her in death in July of two thousand and four. I don't think a day goes by that I don't think of them. I do miss our times together and yet while they are gone from my presence, they are never far away.

Every Christmas Eve I sit up late into the night. For some reason Christmas always brings out nostalgia in me. I love to watch old Christmas movies. I watch midnight mass. I'm not Catholic but I do love the glorious music. When the television goes off, I'll sit and look at the tree. Then, my mind travels back to Christmas' long past. I see the old aluminum tree. There it stands, changing colors as the color wheel turns, covered in glass ornaments. All around the base of the tree are toys. Glorious, wonderful toys. Then, there beside the tree stands mother, alive again. In her hands she holds a beautiful baby doll for my sister. She lifts it high above her head, as if it were a real baby. Suddenly, out of the side of my eye, I detect movement. I turn my head to see seven-year-old me. I am standing, my eyes transfixed on mother, with a confused look on my face. Suddenly, I blurt out "You're not Santa!" Mother was so shocked she tossed the poor baby doll into the air. That baby doll did three somersaults before mother caught her.

"What are you doing out of bed?" She scolded.

"I thought you were Santa and I wanted to say hello." I answered wondering why mother was out of bed.

"Don't you know little children are not supposed to see Santa. Lucky for you, he just left."

Sometimes, I see grandma standing before me. There she stands dressed in her police uniform. Even though I know they are but memories of the past, just the memories make my heart swell with pride.

How well I remember dropping our daughter off at college. My heart was so torn. On the one hand I was so filled with pride. On the other hand, I felt so very sad. That day, I remembered back to when I went off to school. There, stood mother and grandma. They smiled and waved as we backed out of the driveway. Yet, behind those smiles was a pain of heart that I never understood until our Anna went off to college.

Mother and grandma are gone, but they are never far away from me. Life, they say, is a series of goodbyes. The day will come when we bid farewell to our beloved parents. Our children are born to us, they grow up in our presence, like tender plants. Yet, we always know, in the back of our minds, the day will come when they spread their wings and leave us. At some point in life, the till death do us part portion of the wedding vow will come to pass. We say goodbye to a husband or a wife. Family and friends all bid us a fond farewell.

However, as Christians we have something of which the world knows nothing. We have a blessed hope in Christ Jesus. I never said goodbye to my parents. I simply said "until we meet again, where the Son never sets and the rose never fades away. Thanks be to God for such a blessed hope, As I said at the beginning of this book, I was born a fatherless child. But God blessed my sister and I with two extraordinary women. They were by no means perfect, they had their faults as we all do. That is why we need, and have, a Saviour.

When I consider so many fathers who have abdicated their responsibilities to their children I can say, as the women of old said to Naomi, the mother-in-law of Ruth. "For thy daughter-in-law, which loveth thee, which is better to thee than seven sons." Ruth 4:15.

MAMA'S BOY: A YOUNG BOY'S MEMORY OF CHILDHOOD

My mother and grandma, which loved my sister and me, were better to us than seven fathers. Until we meet again, know this, you did good! You are loved and always will be.

Your loving children, Michael and Kathy.

www.ingramcontent.com/pod-product-compliance
Lightning Source LLC
LaVergne TN
LVHW010550070526
838199LV00063BA/4925